LATIN

Ruud Vermey, born 1953 in Den Haag, Holland, is an experienced teacher of Dance, best known among competitive Latin American dancers. Before studying for his Master Degree in Dance Studies at the University of London, he worked internationally in the professional theatre and in the competitive dance world.

He currently runs a Dance Centre in Holland where he coaches and organizes courses for professionals and amateurs.

He lectures and teaches extensively throughout the competitive Latin American dance world and writes articles for international dance magazines.

Ruud Vermey

LATIN

Thinking, Sensing and Doing in Latin American Dancing

Kastell Verlag

ONDERWEG
Institution for Dance Development
Lijsterlaan 1, Alphen a/d Rijn, Holland.
Phone: ++31-1720-707 75 – Fax: ++31-1720-261 87
[New numbers as from September 1995:
Phone: ++31-172-47 07 75 – Fax: ++31-172-42 61 87]

Danceschool Ruud Vermey
Zaalbergstraat 13
2405 XA Alphen a/d Rijn, Holland
Phone: ++31-1720–725 09 (—751 80)
[After September 1995 new numbers:
Phone: ++31-–72-–7 25 09]

P.O. Box 440 312, D–80752 Munich, Germany
Tel. –(0)89–33 21 75 - Fax –(0)89–340 11 78.

Editor and Jacket Design: Christoph Burgauner.
(The jacket is based on a painting by
Krikor Momdjian, owned by the author.)
Printed in Italy by
Legoprint s.r.l., Trento
ISBN 3-924592-44-6

Dedication

This book is dedicated to the Latin American dance institution which has given me the opportunity to put my ideas into practice, and to my pupils who have stimulated me by challenging me constantly and who have always been prepared to take on my ideas and embody them on the dance floor.

Acknowledgments

I am indebted to Walter Laird, my principal Latin American dance teacher during my active dancing career, who influenced my thoughts and ideas on Latin American dancing and provided me with a solid technique on which I could base my future studies.

I am grateful to Dr. Valerie Preston-Dunlop, my tutor in Choreology and Dance Education during my M.A. studies at the Laban Centre for Movement and Dance (London), who believed in my capabilities, stimulated me, and encouraged me to discover a world of dance beyond Latin American dance. I am indebted to the philosophers, writers, choreographers and dance artists whose writings and practice have given me access to that world. I would like to express my thanks to Peter Townsend who, with his understanding of and insights into the controversial issues considered here, has challenged my ideas constantly. His suggestions as a performer and teacher of Latin dance were of great value. My thanks to Yvonne van der Niet, who knew exactly how to give me space to write this book by taking care of all other business arrangements.

My biggest debt is owed to Rosemary Brandt M.A., with whom I endlessly discussed all the topics and who helped to reconstruct each chapter of this book. Finally Christoph Burgauner, the publisher, who had the courage to take on board this book and was more than helpful in giving insights into and suggestions on the text.

Finally, I have to thank all those who helped me to express my ideas and comments in a language which is, despite of being so familiar to me, still a foreign language.

Content

Preface

I never set out to write this book – in a sense it has written itself! My queries and investigations began as a result of a dissatisfaction during my active competitive years in dancing. I knew that dancing was more than a physical activity, but just what else there was to it, I had yet to discover. This marked the beginning of my critical approach to the Latin Dance Institution, the beginning of discoveries, the beginning of an exciting process in which Latin dance was revealed, illuminated, and understood.

Through the further study of dance in general I discovered how much more there is to Latin dance. This book is a concrete way of sharing my discoveries and excitement with all of you who practise Latin American dance and represents my personal commitment to the institution itself.

As an active practitioner in the Latin Dance Institution I am acutely aware of the personal manner of an engagement in the different activities of performing, coaching, teaching, choreographing and judging. Some of my criticisms might feel like a personal attack to some of you, but I urge you to read on and confront them. In no way is the presentation of this material intended personally. Its most important purpose is to invite the reader to enter into the realm of endlessly available material in the world of dance in general and to stimulate a dialogue within the practice, which creates a basis for development and a point of view.

Great dancers, and great teachers have contributed to the development of Latin dance and great dancers and great teachers continue to do so today. This book is not about those people, it is not an appraisal of Latin dance. It is a critical investigation of the practice in an attempt to provide a theory for a practice of Latin dance which can stand on its own in the greater world of dance.

But therefore we need to eliminate in my opinion the self-indulgent attitude towards the use of dance, the exposure of vanity which create empty movement instead of understanding personality embodiment in dance. This lack of coherence makes you feel as if you were looking at branches and leaves without roots.

To some of you the terminology used at times might seem academic and you might be tempted to turn away and return to the business of "doing" rather then reading, i.e. thinking, sensing and reflecting. Through conscious intentional use of the different components of dance the dancers become aware of their communication with the audience; the alternative often results in confusion. Through this book I share what I have experienced as invaluable information and my personal thoughts, although the content is directed towards Latin, the content stands by itself and can be applied to Standard dancing as well.

In any bookstore, library on dance institutions we find publications about dance related to Ballet, Jazz Dance and Modern Dance. In what is called the ballroom danceworld, however, we find mostly videos and popular magazines. The frivolity attached to dance studies in this field might be another reason why Ballroom Dancing – Standard as well as Latin, even when it is performed on a very high level indeed – is quite often not taken seriously.

I strongly believe – and this is the reason why I set out to study things for many years and why I try to present my results in written words – that Ballroom Dancing, once it is taken more seriously, can be improved fom inside and that this is the way to make it more recognized from outside.

Introduction

The material in this book has been handled with the explicit aim that the book be not only readable, but also usable. The structuring of the material and its presentation embodies its primary objective: the separation of the elements in dance from one another not only for the purpose of clarification and identification, but also in order to reinforce the fact that it is impossible to single out any one component of dance without being aware of its interdependency upon other components.

The ingredients of dance, whether they are structural, political, philosophical, institutional or personal have been given clarity through the use of specific terminology. Terminology enables an understanding of the ingredients themselves, the possibility of verbally communicating them to others, and enables an approach to them, specifically in practice, in the dance studio. Their interdependence illuminates the process and the product, the dancing and the dance.

In dance you can choose your ingredients depending on what you want to create. The more ingredients you understand and are familiar with the more choices you have in your creativity. You can achieve complete control of what is perceived, how much of this, less of that, more of the other, etc., provided you understand that the particular combination is the product, the performance. The given ingredients create the final product, and awareness of them illuminates it.

Although I tried hard to investigate and communicate what I had learnt and experienced, I was constantly aware of the fact that no text can ever capture the essence of dance. As Isadora Duncan stated: "If I could tell you what I mean, there would be no point in dancing."

Chapter 1

Competitive Latin American Dance

Ballroom dancing, which includes Standard and Latin American dancing, is offered by dance schools as a social activity. The function of social ballroom dancing is to give physical enjoyment to the participants, through the performance of standardized rhythms and movements, and social satisfaction through group participation. One of the joys of social dancing is the spontaneous element of participation. The concern is not with form. The basic technique provides the vehicle for participants of social Latin dance to release energy and thus express themselves in a physical way in a controlled, supportive, social environment.

This relaxed social dancing environment is the root of competitive Latin American dancing. Today's competitive institution is artificially kept alive. Today's social dances are very different from the ones we are still competing with. It therefore has a life on its own and decisions have to be made on how to develop a danceform which will stand with equal importance next to other more accepted danceforms. Perhaps because it grew out of a social environment, as opposed to an artistic one, it seems to have maintained an isolation from the greater "dance as art" context. In this isolation it emerges with significant elements which characterize not only its practice but the nature of the institution.

The Ambivalence of Competition

The most significant element, which dictates the rules and conventions, and which provides the most common opportunity for the performance of Latin American dance, is "*competition*". Normally, rules and conventions for practice are made by those in authority, and in a hierarchical sense, put into practice. But in this institution the rules and conventions seem to be created by the dancers and teachers themselves. In performance, one dance couple works to outdo another. This same competitive attitude pervades the practice studio. Different teachers teaching private lessons to different dance couples at the same time in the same studio is a common situation. Thus your opponent might have a lesson, not only at the same time, but in the same studio. The place radiates competitiveness. The dancers are competing even while practising, and the behaviour of teachers and dancers is affected by this situation. The style is pushed further. Instead of being involved in the lesson in a manner in which the content of the dance may be experienced, the need to be better than others is explicitly addressed so that this becomes the focus of the dance activity.

Dancers come to lessons in carefully chosen practice outfits which closely resemble performance outfits. Hair is placed and carefully groomed, make-up is immaculate, not only in order to look and feel good but to impress opponents and teachers/judges. Dress regulations for practice or performance have never been laid down in a written document. The development of Latin American dance outfits/costume has been fuelled by both contemporary fashion and the competitive element in the institution. That the institution moulds and attracts personalities is clearly visible in the behaviour and fashion of its participants, but that the practitioners have influenced and indeed moulded the function of the institution and the style of the dancing is less overt.

Coach and/or Judge ?

A problem directly related to the element of competition is the objectivity/subjectivity of those who judge the competitions, i.e. the performances. In many instances the teacher is choreographer, coach, and judge. A genuine learning/teaching situation is more than often disturbed as a result. For a competition programme the teacher/choreographer will give the dancers material which highlights their abilities and which does not require them to expose their weaknesses. A judge will therefore see them at their best. When they seek coaching from a teacher who happens to judge their next competition, will they be more eager to impress than to learn? Such behaviour serves to create and uphold political aspects of the institution.

When the Latin American dancer's aim is only to win, there is no dancing for dancing's sake. In sport the winner's achievements are capable of being more objectively measured, whereas dancers in a competition are at the mercy of the subjective opinions of judges. In a competition, judging is based specifically on the notion of comparison. Assessing twelve couples at the same time on a crowded dance floor with the task of having to select six couples for the final round in a period of one and a half minutes is a "normal" situation. It is tempting for the participants, knowing the short time available for the judges to assess their work, to try to impress them with a dance routine packed with a series of virtuosic tricks. Thus we see the judging format dictate not only the content of the programme, but affect as well the attitude towards and the dynamic quality of the dance itself.

Virtuosity tends to include high energy dynamics such as strength, sudden, speedy movements, direct changes in space and increased tension. Thus programmes tend to be overfilled with these qualities. Dancers also are preoccupied with making sure that they are seen by all judges who are positioned around the dance floor. Thus the floor patterns of the programmes are created with this in mind. Turns are done sometimes to consciously expose the couple's number to the judges, and different heats are performed in different areas of the dance floor to ensure exposure to all judges and most of the audience.

The fact that performance means competition, and that successful dancers gain recognition through winning, undermines the important function of process in the training of the dancers. A teacher will be aware of the process, i.e. the progress of his pupils, and a teacher's assessment of the product will always be formed by a consideration of the process. But judges will mostly observe and consider parts of the product, except of course where competitors are known to them, and this begs the question of whether judges can be so objective as to ignore former knowledge and not be influenced by it.

The only way to overcome this problem would be to insist that judges were not teachers and were external to the training process. But until such a move is taken, the objectivity of judges' decisions will be in question, and thorough and fair assessment will not be possible. The "politics" of the competitive dance situation will continue to thrive and, in doing so, feed the competitive element even more.

Dancers and Persons

That the ultimate performance opportunities for the Latin American dancer are the judged competitions, demands an understanding of the idea of "dance performance." In a theatrical dance work the dancers perform a "role", in other words they do not present themselves. Through this role they, as artists, find opportunities to perform with skill, commitment and artistry. They become the dance. Their Latin American counterparts are presented to their audience by their own name and dance as themselves. People came to see Nurejev *in the role* of Romeo, while in a Rumba we come to see Mr. and Miss Jones. The paradoxical result is the ballroom dancer's inflated ego. The person becomes more important than the dancer, the person becomes more important than the dance. The behaviour of their audience is significantly different from the behaviour of the theatre audience who recognize the theatre as the artist's platform upon which something is to be "created" and where they, as the audience, are spectators. The audience in the competition dance hall participates with as much verve as the dancers. Names of dancers are called out, flags are waved and favourites are cheered and applauded during the "performance." Obviously this affects the end result. For the dancers to rise above themselves, to become the dance in this situation, is difficult. Again, the institution seems to dictate the nature of the dance performance and the dancing experience of the dancers. This need not be the case. The following chapter discusses different choices dancers can make in their approach to competitive dancing.

Approaches to Competitive Dancing

Three Approaches

This chapter identifies three approaches to competitive dance. In the Scandinavian countries, Benelux, Germany and Switzerland, Latin dance appears to be presented as *sport.* Tanzspiegel, a monthly German magazine on Ballroom dance, presents itself as an "Organ des Deutschen Tanzsportverbandes" which means: Magazine of the German dance sport organization. The language used to describe the dancing indicates an acceptance of the Latin dance activity as a sport event. Some sections are headed as follows, "Schweizer Amateur Tanzsport Verband", "Österreichischer Tanzsport Verband", "Tanzsportjugend", "Senioren-Sport." (1)

On the other hand *Dance News*, a weekly newspaper published in the U.K., uses language in article headings such as: "The International at the Royal Albert Hall London," "B.D.F Star Ball in Grovenor House," "Open British in Blackpool Winter Gardens," "A Visit to Grand Hotel Hof Ragaz and Badrutts Palace." Most of the reporting is on national and international competitions and the language used (superlatives and elegant locations) elevate these occasions and present participants as stars. The plethora of advertisements, "World Masters", "United Kingdom Championships (open to the World)", "The Star Ball and Dinner", reinforce the grandeur of these occasions and suggest Latin as elegant *dance* activity related to the world of dance rather than the world of sport. (2)

Dance Beat, a monthly American publication, reports on Ballroom dance activities mainly in America. Numerous photographs of dancing partners showing off the glamour and glitter of their outfits and capturing acrobatic poses fill every page. The language: "Galaxy Ball", "Fiesta Grande Banquet on the River", "The Picnic Garden Party Gala", "Spectacular Floorshows", "The Grand National Dance Festival and Dance Championships" emphasizes the entertainment and "showy" aspects of Latin dance. The platforms for performance do indeed give the dancers opportunities to perform in a "Las-Vegas style". (3)

Given these – three examples, identification of the nature and function of the Latin American dance institution is – problematic.

Some practise it as sport, some as dance loosely related to artistic practice and some as entertainment. Somehow all these approaches are possible. An examination of the features which dominate the practice, when one of the three approaches is used, might reveal something about the institution.

Sport – Art – Show

The term "sport" originates from the Latin "deportare" which literally means "carry away", but in a metaphorical sense means to "relax", to be occupied with something that takes away the seriousness of life and brings freedom, pleasure and enjoyment. Originally sport was pursued as an activity for its own sake. (4) The *Oxford Guide to the English Language* describes sport as: "amusement, fun." For the sake of this discussion, sports such as skating, diving and gymnastics will be considered. Like Latin dancing, they are under subjective *judgement*, and participants are governed by a specific standardized practice and concerned with demonstrating skill.

All artistic practices have their particular medium. The medium of dance is the human body and its movement in tune with music. As a medium, the general characteristics of human expressiveness are retained but are embodied in the dance in such a way as to suggest new meaning. Dance as an art is a created structure which holds new meanings that never existed before, and this new meaning can only be discerned or come into existence for the perceiver when the dance is in-the-making i. e. being carried out. The impact of ideas or intentions on the medium results in their transformation from concept to form, and it is this created form that holds the attention of the spectator.

Showdancing, the kind presented in *Dance Beat*, appears to be preoccupied with elements of display, public exhibition, outward appearance and performance before an audience. Richard Kislan, describes showdance as "a convention of body movement drawn from a variety of sources applied to commercial entertainment for the purpose of amusement". (5) He states too, that the "language of showdancing is not precise" and this can be understood if one examines the institutions that perpetuate showdancing, such as the *Lido* in Paris and *Stardust* in Las-Vegas. Often the dancers are in a sense dehumanized, being used as moving decor, or wearing gigantic costumes while stage effects such as lazers, waterfalls, animals, helicopters, ice-rinks, fires, take over as the spectacle. The audiences are amazed and overwelmed by this "show" while the dance/dancers are overtaken and overcome by the operation of the other strands of this particular medium. Show dancing is commonly seen in musicals as dance numbers interspersed between the songs and narratives and star entertainers are often backed by showdancers.

These comments on "sport", "art", "show" suggest some fundamental differences. In sport the participant could be basically concerned with *winning*, in art with *creating* and in show with *displaying*. Thus each approach has its particular aim or intention. In sports the dominating *aim* is to win, by doing well what has to be done. A particular act has to be performed. The way in which the activity is carried out is of central importance. The *intention* of the performer of these acts is a practical one. Sport is a "purposeful physical activity". (6) The fulfillment of these functions is a "completely absorbing vital activity", enjoyable perhaps aesthetically, but while the operation is going on there is no time to dwell upon aesthetic qualities. (7) If the desire to win is the ingredient in the purpose of the activity, aesthetic qualities of sport are only by-products. (8)

If we agree that the aim of the sports person performing a particular act is related to the practical purpose of winning, we might suggest that the aim of the artist in creating something, is related to an aesthetic purpose.

When the aesthetic attitude is taken up or evoked by the dancer we attend to the forms of what we perceive in a different way; the forms themselves come to have a "special sort of meaningfulness". (9) This is the contemplative aesthetic attitude which exists in an aesthetic situation. Thus the aim of the artist is aesthetically motivated.

Intention and Performance

So the aim/intention of the dancer artist is not simply to create a form, but to sustain the "living-through experience" of the dance in its full concreteness so that it can be enjoyed aesthetically. (10) In other words, the dancer is aware that the dance being created by virtue of its being performed has no existence other then during those moments in which it is performed. Once the dance is over its special sort of meaningfulness might be reflected upon by those who perceived it, but its concreteness is only available for perception during its making, during its performance.

There are two aspects that are helpful in attempting to suggest the show dancer's intention/aim and which provide insight into the special problems of that concept known as popular commercial art. The first is the social perception of art itself. In his book *Culture* (1981), Raymond Williams suggests that there is a historical development of systems of social signals which indicate what is or is not to be regarded as art. The most common kinds of signal are those of "occasion" and "place." The signal of an art gallery is obvious because it is so established and conventional that it hardly has to be noticed. We absolutely understand the paintings in the gallery to be works of art, but the painting on a house wall lacks the expected signal, and we are immediately uncertain whether it is intended as art or not. Likewise musicals staged in London's West End Theatres provide popular entertainment, different from the ballet or opera productions staged at the Royal Opera House or Covent Garden. The place/venue signals the intention. The dancer/performer at *Stardust*, Las-Vegas has a different intention from her/his counterpart of the New York City Ballet at the New York City Center.

The point is that the show dancer's intention is different from the artist dancer's intention by virtue of signals that support the activity. Raymond Williams' second signal is "presumed value". He gives the example that cinema films are commercial popular culture but that some films are considered "high art". (11) Opera, ballet and contemporary theatrical dance performances attract members of society who are engaged in these art practices and those who enjoy engaging in comtemplating philosophies, theories, issues etc. In art these are generally presented to be enjoyed as an aesthetic experience, or merely to challenge expectations and perceptions of what that experience might be. This is not considered popular entertainment nor even entertainment and, by virtue of that division, falls into Raymond Williams' category of "high-art". However show dancing itself clearly falls into the "popular art" category because it has a wider audience, is widely enjoyed/liked and in its presentation intends to entertain. Competitive Latin dance has a large following world-wide and is popular within many different cultures and societies. According to Williams, Latin dance seems to fall into the popular art category.

The Latin American dancer can certainly adopt any one of the approaches discussed, which means that the dance will be created by the intention/aim adopted. Dancers approaching a competition performance with what might be called a "sport-attitude" will dance to win, with a purposeful physical activity, fulfilling the act as perfectly as possible to elicit the best result. An artist's approach to a competition performance means that the dancers take the functional physical activity of their routines and consciously and deliberately create something that will be felt and perceived as aesthetic expressive forms. If the dancers adopt a show approach, the form of the dance routine becomes less significant and the self is displayed and exhibited. Their intention is to win using the movement as a vehicle to present themselves in the most popular way and provide their audience with entertainment.

Impact on Expression

Another point worth considering is how expression might function when dance is approached in the three different ways.

Expression in sport activities has nothing to do with the performance of the act. The sports person may express feelings of "aggression, triumph or sheer animal spirits," but it would be wrong to say sport *is* that expression. The expression of the sports person is a private one which has to do with private feelings and the attitude related to the situation, it has no function in sport. (12)

In show dance there is a tendency to "put on a face". This ties in with the aim/intention to entertain, to top each preceding number with a better, cleverer, trickier, more spectacular razzle-dazzle performance. Show dancing puts a lot of emphasis on sheer athleticism (tricks) which Richard Kislan considers to be a necessary part of the dancers repertoire. Thus a show dance approach to Latin dancing would stress the acrobatic, athletic tricks as a means of *impressing* audience rather then as a means of expression. The form is thus devoid of expressive content, so the dancer adopts facial expressions to go with the tricks.

An artistic approach to Latin dancing might allow the dancers to differentiate between the expression embodied in the form of their rumba sequence and that expression embodied in the form of their jive sequence. An artist's approach does not allow the separation of technique from expression. The technique is the means with which the expression is transformed and embodied in the medium.

The line between sport and art is difficult to draw. Dancing is more readily accepted as art, but is all dancing art? Are gymnastics and skating art? Is the judge of the gymnastic championship or the Latin American competition judge concerned with assessing genuine artistic and expressive qualities or are they judging efficiency and functional perfections of the movement?

Skill, Craft and Art

This introduces the notion of skill and craftsmanship. Essentially there is a close relationship between good artists and good craftsmen, but as R. Collingwood points out, there is an important conceptual difference: "The craftsman carries out a predefined plan, whereas the artist discovers in the making." (13)

The dominating motive of the artist would be to produce a form for aesthetic contemplation. A sports person whose skill could never be denied, would concentrate on carrying out the predefined plan while addressing interest in strategy and tactics. The artist would concentrate on producing a form which would represent something other than what is being performed, expressing interest in what is being created by virtue of what they are actually doing.

An important distiction between the skill of the sports person and the skill of the artist is that the artist's skill is "assimilated into his art". (14) Thus the performing Latin dancer may move with perfected technical skill, but if he is a *dancer artist*, skill alone will not make him so. Of course, it must be acknowledged that all three approaches require skill and that in Latin American competitive dancing as such there are "artistic elements" and aspects, but this does not qualify it to be called "art". (15)

The competition in Latin American dance is the frame, the occasion which provides performers with opportunities to focus on skill. The invention of the competition is the very structure which has given the institution its identity and is responsible for the diversity of approaches within its practice. Finally, it remains for the dancer to adopt either of these three approaches and to understand their differences, so that they can be in control of their performances.

Sport	Art	Show
Aim		
winning	creating	displaying
Intention		
practical purpose	aesthetic purpose	entertainment
purposeful physical activity	result: forms have special sort of meaningfulness and sustain the illusion	– popular
	the living-through experience	
Expression		
private	aesthetic expression embodied in the form of the dance	impressive rather than expressive
		facial expression
		self expression
Skill		
related to strategy in carrying out a predefined plan	assimilated into the work	similar to sport
		physical tricks
Outcome / result		
a winner a result	present a form	present yourself

Competition

The notion of success and the pressure of achievement is a very real one in the Latin American dance institution. The question is whether what is seen as success is really experienced as such. Does success mean winning? In a competition of 500 competing couples are there really 499 "losers"? Is 1st place, and the value given to it, so important that all other results and experiences by all competitors are considered unsuccessful? All the striving to get "there", to improve, to develop, involves a deep and often heartfelt physical and emotional journey, a process of growth. Does success have anything to do with this process? And if so, where in the functioning of the institution is such success given value and recognition? What is more important? The achievement itself or the meaning of success, the title or what was learned along the way? Again, there are titles and titles. The most valued is a world title – "the best in the world".

I am suggesting that the platform, the achievement, winning, the product function differently from the way personal aims function within the same notion of success. A dancer who is "busy with winning" needs to be clear about how that affects his attitude to dancing. Clarity concerning the reason for striving will give deeper meaning to success. It is just possible that the value of success really lies in the getting there and not in the moment of glory.

Competition dancing is not like a theatre performance where all the strands of the medium are allowed to function as planned and practised, where the dancers expectations can usually be rooted in a previous experience. Latin competitors have to deal with a different situation. Besides preparing their programme for performance through practice, training and coaching, there are elements of the performance that cannot be anticipated and need to be dealt with "on their feet". Space is sometimes insufficient, new directions have to be taken on the "spot", the dancing sometimes has to stop in time and space because the couples have become "hemmed in", a figure cannot be performed as planned because of lack of space. Competitors never know what music is going to be played, nor do they know when it will stop, and therefore they often have to choreograph an ending on the spot.

All competitive occasions bring with them a special energy and excitement that can freeze the dancer into "stage fright". Or this unique sense of occasion can serve to stimulate the dancers. Coping with the unexpected conditions on the dance floor, with the nervous energy which one minute might support you and the next shake you off balance and out of control, with your partner's nervous energy, with the technical challenges in your programme – all this can be a very daunting experience. Indeed one wonders why dancers compete at all, and certainly we admire their courage or foolhardiness. In such situations, what do you concentrate on? You can often feel the energy of the challenge in the dancers next to you and all around you. Do you keep one eye on them and one eye on your own performance? Certainly this experience is not like the experience of the practice occasion.

Is it possible to practise these competitive situations in order to prepare oneself more fully for all the physical, intellectual, emotional and social behavioural demands that are made on the dancers simultaneously? It seems reasonable to suggest that a clear strategy to cope with this situation might be imperative for each couple to adopt, so that the dancing itself gets a chance to be perceived on the competition floor.

This strategy involves deciding whether the primary focus will be "competing" or will be on the dance and dancing. A competitive spirit is valuable, but not if it is the only aim. It could work against one. Dancers who use their programme to compete or as a vehicle for presenting a challenge, all too often lose their dancing, lose their partnership, and the whole activity looks like a high-powered struggle, whereas those who can concentrate on the dancing itself present the dance as something to be enjoyed, valued, assessed, enjoying a completely different experience.

When the attitude or approach to the dancing is only goal oriented, the movement is done differently because the dancer who is the movement, who is doing the dancing, has a primary and real emotional concern which is motivating him or her and which has very little or nothing to do with the motivation behind the choreography. This leads to a confusing situation for both the dancers and the audience. Fighting to reach a position is not one of the choices I recommend, because it can never serve the dancing.

So often the "competitive spirit" encourages the ego to become involved, to seek satisfaction. Should the competition be a platform for the dancers to create dance or promote themselves? When the dancers are "superior" top professionals, should they present "superiority" or superior dancing? I suggest that if the situation is not being controlled by the dancers in a conscious and skilful way, i.e. they have a clear strategy, the dancers come across as arrogant and separated from the dance.

The Mirror on the Wall

Another reason a lot of dancers can so easily become preoccupied with their ego is the use of mirrors in studios. Mirrors are helpful devices in that a dancer can see the shape or form of their bodies, can see and check the shape or form of their movements in relationship to their partner's and can check to see what aspects of their dance movements might look like. The negative effect might relate to how the use of mirrors encourage a preoccupation with what they look like, reinforcing a sense of self-approval from the outside. When the mirror is taken away, confidence drops and the movements are devoid of power, sense and meaning.

It is important to be able to create the form without looking in the mirror. To internalize and visualize what a correct line feels like and to be able to store that feeling in order to reproduce it is what is required of the dancer. If using a mirror is the only way dancers can know or feel this correctness, preoccupation with the mirror tends to become a focus point outside the body and remains a reflection apart from what is a true movement experience.

Is it not wise to assess the actualities and elements of each competitive occasion, the energy, the hype, the atmosphere (is it sophisticated, electric, casual, bristling with tension, etc.), the judges and what they mean to you, who the competitors are, who your close competitors are, the music, the size of the "auditorium" and audience? And then let all this information inform and prepare you for your performance, rather than disturb you. Why should competitors feel that by disparaging others they promote themselves? Why should a competitor feel that being placed higher than another makes the other a lesser person? "Your enemies are not those about you in the studio, but your own imperfections. You can't fight yourself if you run away and refuse to see yourself." (1)

The negative aspects of competition need to be acknowledged and thought through if competitive dancing is going to perpetuate the kind of dancing that the dance world, beyond the Latin world, will admire. The kind of dancing that these negative aspects produce is fighting energy, exaggerated stereotypes, exaggerated and peculiar facial expressions, tortured, anxious manipulations of the body, overtly sexual dress. All this and a level of tension that has no place in social dance, go towards creating a spectacle of competitive Latin dancing that is in danger of being considered funny, insincere and "over the top". It is a pity that those couples in the top ranks who are very skilful performers indeed and do have the ability to bring to Latin dance – without losing the special and positive excitement of the competition event – the distinction and recognition both it, and they, deserve, very rarely are fully recognized in the wider arena of dance performance. I think something has to be done about it – and can be done.

Exposure and Overexposure

Other aspects of competition which serve to dictate its function and assesment are its duration and its production element. To participate in a competition, dancers have to dance in several "rounds", not always knowing which is their last and how many more they will participate in. The impact of the dancer on the audience in the theatre is somehow supported by the amount and kind of exposure the dancers endure. Dancing your way through a three act ballet or through a twenty minute work is easier than repeating your same five dances, five times, on the same night, to the same audience. This overexposure is hard to sustain and works against the Latin dancer. Instead of the climax being in the dance performance as it is for the theatre dancer, the climax in competition is the production, and couples are just cogs in the wheel. By the final round the dancing has already been seen several times, the impact has come and gone. *The results* are what the event is all about.

The positive aspect of competition is that each competition is its own unique occasion, each round becomes another opportunity, a new assessment, a new mental setting. This newness, the constant "re-creation" of the new event is what builds the energy, builds excitement. It is the occasion and all its built-in structures that hold it together, not the individual dancer's energy and tension. Each dancer is a small but unique part of the whole.

The Question of Authenticity

Competitive Latin dance, as we know it today, has its roots in the conventions and traditions derived from the social and cultural life of Cubans and Brazilians of the 1930's, the Spanish of the 1920's and North Americans of the 1940's. The Rumbas and Sambas of this time captured things which were meaningful and significant for that particular society and culture. You will, of course, never see a Cuban Rumba or Brazilian Samba until you travel to the birthplace.

For a variety of reasons, like the presence of American soldiers in Europe during the second World War, the development of technology, music from records, radio, television and film, the social dancing of one ethnic group was transplanted into other cultures. Thus the ethnic dances of the Cubans, Brazilians etc. found their way into North American and European cultures, and there they became influenced by the behaviour and moral and social values of the adoptive culture. But through transplantation into other cultures original motivation and primal cause are lost and dance then loses its true essence.

John Martin writes: "It is far easier to speak in a foreign language without a trace of an accent than it is to dance a foreign idiom with complete purity of style." (1)

The beginning of the distinction between popular dance and social dance is marked historically by the foundation of the Official Board of Ballroom Dancing in England in 1929. The Board aimed at standardizing the dance movements and vocabulary of their adopted popular dances, thus creating a technique for social dance. This led to the regulation of dance competitions, a further transplantation from the social dance situation to the competition dance floor.

At the current stage of its evolution and development, Latin American dance is far removed from its original sources and motivations. Today, the English standardized International Style is characterized by an erect and elegant posture in the rumba, legs and feet "placed" with knees straightened and the arms "placed". In all five dances the focus is outwards. Presentation is also enhanced by increased travelling around the dance floor. The dance hold has lost its intimacy in its preoccupation with correctness. An examination of ethnic Latin dances will reveal an inner focus which enhances physicality and sensuality. The dance hold creates the framework for the intimacy of partnership, the arm movements serve to balance the body in motion, the vertical posture is alive with undulating movements while the weight encounters gravity in a relaxed physical sense, creating sensuous curving body shapes and movements.

It is obvious and understandable that the International Style of Latin American dance is English in character. It was standardized there, on English dancers by English teachers. It is interesting to note how many English couples have been World Champions. The dances are accompanied by the arrangements and compositions of Victor Sylvester, Ross Mitchell and Edmundo Ross. Afternoon tea dance entertainment is a far cry from the improvised, syncopated sounds of Caribbean musicians, deep throated negro songs, throbbing guitars and whispering crooners.

Today it is not only the English who are dancing the accepted International Style. As its name implies, the whole world is doing it, conforming to it from the milieu of their own social, cultural and national backgrounds. The style is being pushed further away from its ethnic roots by the influences of the diversity of the world's dancers, teachers and choreographers who must adopt it. La Meri in *Total Education in Ethnic Dance* gives a grave warning: "To depart from authenticity, one must know authenticity very well. One must understand not only the authentic forms but also the motivations, or else one loses the essence of ethnicity, and the result is a mishmash." (2)

This mishmash must be of questionable value. I am not suggesting that there is no place for English influence in Competitive Latin American dance style, nor am I saying that some formal standardization is wrong. The point is, should I go to London, Holland or Cuba to learn the authentic Rumba? Since standardization, development is becoming so manipulated that soon, if not already, we will have a dance style which does not refer to anything else but itself, because it will bear little or no relation to its authentic ethnic roots.

My plea is that those practising competitive Latin dancing today (dancers, teachers, choreographers, judges) be aware of the ethnic sources of this style of dance. Generally today's approach to steps and technique divorces Latin dance from its ethnic sources. An understanding of the individuality will help embue today's style with the richness of the past. In this way we can develop a style which to some degree refers to the significance of the cultural source, a style which will provide traditions and conventions for a creative performance and appreciation of its dances today.

Chapter 2

INSTITUTIONAL STRUCTURES

Audience / Performer Relationship

There is a vast difference between the audience at a competitive dance event and a theatre audience. Most of those who comprise the competitive audience are family, friends, fans and fellow competitors who have come to watch and give support to the competitors. The theatre audience comprises members of the public who have come to witness an artistic performance. They go to see the work itself, the dance performance of Petipa/Ivanov's *Swanlake* or Balanchine's *Serenade*. Although some of the artists may be known to members of the audience, they do not engage with them personally during the performance. Information is given in the programme, names of dancers are given, parts/roles they play are specified, but during the performance, although we "see" the work through their concrete presence, it is the *work* we perceive and with which we commune. This particular relationship separates the performers from the audience, as does the physical structure of the theatre, with the audience in the auditorium in the dark and dancers on the stage. This space is changed and created through lighting etc. It is not possible for a dancer to make personal contact with a member of the audience. If they do the dance is lost.

Yet in the competitive event dancers are introduced as themselves, "Johan and Nadia Eftedal from Norway". They share the large space of the hall with their audience, although the dance floor is clearly defined, but contact with members of the audience is often made through proximity and eye focus. Once this is done, personal contact is made and we see *people* dancing, not the dance itself. In other words there is little distance between dancers and audience on these occasions.

The aim of this chapter is to raise the following questions:

- What is being judged: the people dancing or the dance itself?
- Are the expectations of the audience and judges dictating how the dancers dance?

- Could the dancers control how the dance is perceived and change their relationship between themselves and the audience?
- What would this do for competitive Latin American dance?

There is always a kind of mystery about great dancers who have that special connection with the audience. It seems to always include sincerity. But what is sincerity and how is it recognized? It could be said that when dancers are absolutely committed to what they are doing/making, it also allows a commitment to the way that particular dance functions at that particular time. It is often evident that dancers are occupied with an expression that has nothing to do with the dance. This noncommitment changes the manner in which it is performed.

There are three distinct approaches to competitive Latin dance in practice today. The approaches of artist, sports person or show dancer are discussed in chapter 1. Obviously each approach invites a distinct response, but the point of this discussion is to acknowledge an important aspect of human connection at work regardless of the approach.

Aesthetic Response

Rudolf Laban believed that our kinesthetic sense, related to our unique sense of touch, brings a physical nature to our perceptions. He writes that we are stimulated by bodily activity which gives rise to an awareness of the sensation of the body. Thus the kinesthetic sense as a source of information is vital for the appreciation and the performance of dance. The significance of this notion for Latin American dance lies in the fact that the dancer is seen as a unit of human capacity, related to our being in the world with its communal and social dimensions. The audience and judges are not immune from this experience; they feel the movement of the dancer in their own bodies, they leap and turn with the dancer, they sense their sustainment in time, feeling and knowing the control and release of energy as it occurs in the dancers' body movement. We say that the audience has been stimulated kinesthetically. They are feeling and sensing what the dancers are feeling and sensing dynamically and in so doing they identify with the dancers.

Dance as art is a form of expression. It is intended to be received by other people. In the theatre the dance produced is an art object. It has observable form. The dancers are the material form not separable from the "thing" perceived as the dance. In other words, the audience sees the dance and its living form through the concrete presence of the dancers. (1)

With this view of the communal aspect of dance in the theatre Fraleigh also confirms the kinesthetic and physical nature of the audience's perceptions. It also hints at a deeper experience, the aesthetic experience. When the Latin dancer is creating something for our perception, compared to the theatrical dancer's process of manipulation of, and commitment to the movement, we not only attend to the kinesthesia but we are invited to perceive *"the dance"* aesthetically which involves *more* than merely empathizing with the particular dancer's physical activity.

These aesthetic responses are related to what is "expressed" and these are normally known and understood by impressions retained by the senses when the dance is over. However, if in Latin dancing the ego of the dancer intrudes, i.e. if the movement is worn like a decoration adorning the outer surface, then the "vision" is cluttered and the audience can no longer clearly see *"the dance"*.

Therefore, although kinesthetic empathy may be common to both responses, the audience/performer relationahip is, dependent on the dancer's intention. A successful dance moves the dancer and the audience towards one another. They find a common ground, where the dance is successful and accessible for both. The dancer and the audience come together for just this purpose.

Technique

You can execute movement which is technically correct but still not dance. Hanya Holm writes: "The problem is, if you are not technically proficient enough to perform something simple, you try to cover up that deficiency by doing something complicated to make it more exciting and worthwhile. But this is not good dancing. It is not necessary to get complicated in order to find something of value. There are simple Czerny exercises for pianists, composed expressly to develop dexterity and ease of the fingers. To one person they are just exercises and will sound just like that, but when another person plays them they become beautiful music. In both instances the music was the same. The performance makes the difference." (1)

There are many debates on technique, what it is, what purpose it serves. Is it dancing itself? Is it a tool? Is it the dancer? Is it you? Is it the dance? It is not my purpose here to say what it is, but to offer some views and thoughts for your own assimilation and conclusions.

Technique mostly is seen as something separated from expression in dance. In most dance training, technique is understood as the clear demonstration of the thing to be done, and the taught element is skill. There are terms in each dance style which are instructions for the delivery of specifically named movements or steps. All dance styles have their particular requirements. For example ballet's vertical stance and turn-out, Latin American's dance posture, its horizontal flexible movement and sensing of weight. To achieve these specific requirements practice becomes essential. The learner has to engage in a regular routine of rigorous practice to attain and maintain the strength and flexibility necessary for the physical execution of the vocabulary which increases in volume and difficulty as training progresses.

Practice needs supervision by a teacher, thus we arrive at the concept of "technique training" as the essential learning process. While it is understandable that there is this emphasis on the acquisition of skill in training, it is because of this preoccupation with a perfectly exact delivery of a vocabulary that expression is ignored and separated from technique altogether. Unfortunately, all too often we witness facial expression added to technical skill as an arbitrary accompaniment. Emotional integrity is then in question. The surface does not cohere to the inside; we witness a conflict.

Many writers agree that if the attention becomes too focussed on technique, the action ceases to be expressive and becomes uninspired. Also, struggling with the technique, the steps, the body, results in insufficient shaping and inarticulated expression. Ellfeldt quotes Pauline Koner: "As I have watched the development of dance, in all areas, in all styles, I have seen that there is a greater and greater emphasis on technique, but less and less thought on artistry. I do not mean to imply that technique is not important. It is more and more important, to give the dancer mastery and control. But the most important thing about technique is to have the ability to hide the technical facility, to perform with so much ease that none of the technical difficulties are obvious." (2)

For the performer technique is more than mere display. When your technique arrives at a point where movement becomes automatic you can move beyond just *doing* movement to making something through the movement. Then it is possible for your audience to come closer to having an aesthetic experience, that is for them to be transported into a created world and not only to be impressed by your physical display. On such occasions the dancers' technique, their control of body and movement in all its complexity, serves to create a visible relationship, an image, a symbol, an expression, a conflict etc., for the audience's perception. The dancers and their technique become the dance. The "what" of technique should not be separated from the "how".

Technique is sometimes viewed as the vehicle which gives you access to crafting, to manipulating movement to find expression. There is no such thing as too much technique if the purpose is sincere and appropriate.

Technique can be said to be the foundation of a dancer's potential movement range. All dance styles are generated by selected human movement principles and by being proficient in one of these styles, for example Latin American, Classical Ballet, Modern Jazz. This provides a dancer with a basis, a point of departure into new styles while at the same time serving as a protector of style. Without technique there would be no Latin American competitive style.

In the competitive Latin American world, dancers find themselves travelling long distances and performing day after day, round after round. On some of these occasions mere technical expertise gets them through, while the more desired centered approach is sacrificed under these conditions. So a developed technique can help dancers cope better with the occupational hazards of their lifestyle.

It is commonly acknowledged among dance theoreticians that technical skill in itself is not yet dance. The dancer may know the formula for execution (steps) and the rules upon which that formula is based (straightening, the legs, settling in the hips) but until the dancer can "speak the language in a manner not expressly provided for in the rules, they can make no significant utterance in it". In other words the dancer needs to *know* both the rules and all that must go on in the space between the rules and then have the actual ability to put that knowledge into effect, with skill, before dance can happen. This is learning how to explicitly transform movement vocabulary into dance.

Judging

This chapter is not an attempt to define the activity of judging in competitive Latin dance, but rather an attempt to raise questions about judging which are inherent in the institution. This investigation reveals institutional, political and educational issues, raises further questions pertaining to rethinking the notion of judges, judging and competition itself within competitive Latin dance.

Generally in Latin American dance an adjudicator is described as a person able to give authoritative opinion and is therefore appointed to decide who is going to win the contest. This description implies that judging involves more than individual taste, more than personal opinion. Judging has two spheres, two tasks, one which explicates (knows factually) and the other which evaluates (estimates the worth or value of). The first phase of explication is founded on understanding and knowledge and involves the more objective factual observation of what is there. The second phase, a more subjective phase of evaluation, includes taste, liking and more or less personal predelections. Both phases are interdependent and inter-related.

In competitive Latin dance today those people judging competitions are themselves teachers, coaches and organizers of competitions and often ex-champions. Judging is not a separate occupation or activity confined to the few. This is not to say that those teachers, coaches, organizers etc. who are judging today are people who are unable to give an authoritative opinion. Indeed the very activities of teaching and coaching are those which inform objectively. The problem lies in the fact that dancers can choose to go to certain judges for coaching, not necessarily because they believe them to be good teachers but as a political move. Being a judge institutionally and politically elevates individuals. Somehow judges are given power by competitors, somehow teachers can use their position as judges in the teaching/coaching situation. This is all part and parcel of the politics of competition, but how does it affect the institution in terms of the actual dancing, the results, the position of winner and the notion of real success? Is competition dancing really so deeply rooted in politics, with true value and the merit of the dancing taking a back seat?

Criteria

This is not a direct attack on judges nor on our institution. My concern is to protect both judges and their activity and the value of dancing and dancers within the institution. This can be done through an examination of two different sets of criteria, those which are met by individuals as qualifications for becoming a judge and those which are used in the consideration of value and merit on the dance floor. Firstly, it appears that in most cases individuals have to be in possession of certain diplomas before they can officially judge a competition. These diplomas are loosely related to Latin American dance technique. In the second case it is clear that there are no obvious criteria set down for all judges to share. Individuals have their personal and idiosyncratic formulae for arriving at assessments.

With so few set criteria laid down for qualification and consideration of merit and worth on the dance floor, subjective evaluations thrive, giving little chance for objective evaluations. The politics generated by the teacher/judge situation mentioned earlier further serves subjective evaluation. While judges might not see more than ten seconds of a couple dancing at one time on the competition dance floor, as teachers or observers in other competitions they have seen the whole programme before. Judges know and are familiar with the dance programmes of professional dancers through television appearances, coaching, and watching and judging competitions. So when does the judging begin? Are the dancers really being judged solely on their performance at that time, on that single occasion? As teachers, can judges divorce themselves from the dancers as people they know and judge the dancing on that one occasion? Does the judgment, the evaluation, subconsciously or unconsciously begin in the studio or in the previous competition? Are judges influenced by preconceived ideas about the dancers? Are couples advantaged or disadvantaged because of judges' expectations born in the classroom, the coaching session? Is it at all possible for judges to be totally objective in their evaluations?

Totally objective evaluations are not possible where people are evaluating other people. But I would be bold enough to suggest that, while the unconscious judging cannot be controlled, an outline of what the conscious judging should be about would be advantageous to all concerned, and would uphold institutional values and merit. I suggest that knowledge of historical issues, traditional and institutional issues, aesthetics, technique and style, dance ingredients and components, i.e. knowledge of the context within which Latin Dance appears and knowledge of the intrinsic structures of Latin Dance, should form the prerequisite education for qualification to judge. This education will clearly reveal the context and content of Latin American Dance and in doing so will carry and clarify its own values.

"Each context within which dance appears carries its own values. Social dances are not valued for the same kinds of reasons as ritual dance nor ritual and social dances for the same reasons as theatre dance". (1)

If all judges have the same point of departure, share an awareness of the conventions and traditions of Latin American dance it is more likely that they will share the norms, standards and criteria (implicit in those conventions and traditions) as to what constitutes a dance of value. Once these general standards are in place, a flexibility can be allowed which may give freedom to teachers and dancers but still move towards establishing distinctive values.

As Janet Adshead puts it: "Thus each dance embodies and reflects the values of a given society (or group within a society), a given choreographer and given performers, and they can be judged for their worth in terms of merit, goodness or greatness according to whether and how they manifest the given values." (2)

The concepts through which evaluations/judgements are made are complex, but what I have tried to point out is that it cannot be enough for an individual to pass judgement on a dance or specific dancer's dancing a specific dance, simply by stating what they personally value. Evaluation/judgement is wholly different from attributing personal value to something.

In Latin American dance, the notion of technique is given priority. Technique is set out on paper, is taught with that same exactness and dryness and initially at a level far below that which is ultimately aquired by top performers. By this time dancers are using technical skill as a vehicle for expressing their specific dance in order to give it back text-book style. As a result, to have "technique" as the only tangible and shared criterion among judges would be rather a thin foundation for the establishment of worth, value and merit in the professional field of Latin American dance.

Scenery

The unique relationship that exists, and is generated at a competition, on the dance floor, between judges and dancers, is interesting to examine. Aspects of this relationship are rooted in political strategy and are manifested in the behaviour of both judges and dancers alike. This serves to generate and perpetuate the institution as we experience it. Unlike the theatre, there is no strict division or barrier between those dancing and those perceiving and judging. Judges are placed *on* the dance floor, albeit on the periphery. They are just as much "on stage", in view, as the dancers. Some judges walk around the floor, others remain where they are. It is sometimes clearly visible who the judges are watching or following or returning to, how they observe, how long they observe or whether they observe at all. This behaviour is of significant interest to spectators and dancers.

In a sense, judges are more in view and "on stage" than competitors, as they remain there throughout the different heats, for a sustained period of time. What would it do for the competitors, for the dancers and judges, if the judges were collectively placed "off-stage", separate from the dance floor and dancers, giving over the dance arena to the dance only? How would it affect the competition if their behaviour was not so overt and their specific activity separated and concentrated within a confined area?

Another aspect of the dancers/judges relationship is generated by "open judging". On such occasions we can be sure that there is no intimidation experienced by judges on the dance floor when they have to hold up their authoritative opinion in the form of a "number" for all to see. On these occasions, are not the judges themselves being judged and thus preoccupied with personal politics? Can they become intimidated or influenced by other judges' decisions, or by dancers on the floor? And what effect does "open judging" have on the dancers? Audiences are certainly affected by these results and become involved in the competition. In such cases, does the "competition" take over the dancing? Do the judging and the judge become the central concern? Is it fair or indeed respectful towards the dancers to constantly get this kind of "comment" on their performance, be it positive or negative, before they have finished with their performance?

Even if open judging is done after the performance, public comment on the dancer's performance brings up a crucial educational issue in the area of competition judging/assessment.

Considering the competition situation and all the political aspects at play, it is quite understandable and feasible to suggest that judges arrive at their "results" in highly individual ways. Considering that no one judge will be able to watch one couple's Samba from beginning to end, considering too, that a judge could be the coach/teacher and choreographer of a couple's Samba, considering too that in that role he may be acutely aware of that couple's progress or lack thereof (i.e. personal achievements or failures), we can rightly suggest that whole dances are seldom evaluated, that judges are put in a position of evaluating their own choreography and teaching compared with that of others, and that judges can hardly remain objective or immune to being impressed or surprised by the development of certain couples.

So what is being judged? And has the institution developed in such a way that judges are put in the position of evaluating where any chance of objectivity is impossible? In order to validate the competition itself, to give validity to the act of judging, the success of winning or being placed, and indeed to validate competitive Latin dance at all, it might be necessary to examine the structure of evaluations and the procedure for making them.

Substantiation

Janet Adshead suggests that every evaluation has three important aspects:

1. It relies upon values which may be explicit or implicit.
2. It makes a judgement of worth based upon these values.
3. And it includes a substantiation for the judgement. (3)

These three aspects determine the validity and appropriateness of any evaluation.

The first two aspects have already been discussed, but the third aspect of substantiating a judgement is particularly interesting to consider because of its educational implications. If judges were given the opportunity to reflect on their evaluations made on the dance floor and perhaps to share these reflections with their colleagues on that particular occasion, these discussions could lead to collective substantiation for those couples in the final. In turn, this kind of feedback would be invaluable for couples and allow them to reflect on how their performances are perceived and received, and give them opportunity to make choices and decisions in the light of this feedback. Comparative judging requires ranking dancers relative to one another. But how valuable is a mere number or rank? Placement does not imply good or bad or reveal what judges think and how they arrive at their final decision. Judging requires that value or merit be attributed to the dancing of the couples themselves. In such evaluative judging the rank order or placements emerge from the results and are therefore more objective.

The advantages of value judgements are threefold. Firstly, attention can be directed to the evaluation of the components, ingredients, structures and form of the dance, which could be judged for their correctness, effectiveness, success and appropriateness. (4) Secondly, the execution of these dances can be further evaluated as having merit, goodness or greatness and once those are singled out, further comparative judgements can be substantiated by focussing on differences and on similarities upon which one dance may be said to be better or best. Thirdly, evaluation can focus, in Ashead's words, on "interpretation, that is, on the value of the dance in terms of character, quality or meaning it is seen to bring into existence". (5)

If judged for appropriateness, effectiveness and success, these judgements can be substantiated by pointing out those characters and qualities with reference to the components and their structure. On these grounds dances may be evaluated individually in terms of merit, or they may be evaluated comparatively and said to be better than another or the best of a group.

With a procedure like this in place, judges would find themselves in dialogue with one another, substantiating their judgements, sharing their differing observations and tastes, upon which their personal decisions were made. Actual ranks would be the result of the individual decisions in collected form. The results or ranks would then reflect the general values of that group of people, the values within that tradition and convention and style of dance, and these values would then relate to the purpose of the dance or the particulars of the choreography or performance. The scrutinizer would still gather the individual judge's results and no dialogue would be necessary until after the results had been finalized.

This kind of attention and discussion would encourage a more objective approach to judging and ensure that at all times it is the dance that is the focus of all comments and evaluation. Specific feedback can only be welcomed by dancers and audience and serve to inform and educate the public in a way which would enhance the appeal and validity of competitive Latin American dance as an institution.

Chapter 3

Expression – Feeling – Emotion

In Latin dance these three terms are often used interchangeably, presuming they are all referring to the same thing. This lack of caution can cause misunderstandings and confusion and, on the part of the user, could indicate a lack of responsibility. The following discussion attempts to define the differences between these terms and in so doing will encourage the reader to come to his/her own more refined understanding of what they mean.

The term emotions refers generally to states of the mind caused by confrontations with realities. We do not become angry, happy or sad without a reason. These states are part of our life experience. *Feelings*, on the other hand, can be said to be a mental or physical awareness of these emotions. You have a temper due to your anger, you become weak through laughing.

Expression is the manifestation of either emotions or feelings. We do not see feelings, we do not see emotions but we see them *expressed* in some form. That form is what we call expression.

The emotion of anger may be felt by somebody but with no intention of being expressed or communicated to others. On the other hand, *being angry* with someone is expressed or communicated via the verbal and non-verbal channels. In this way anger is given form, i.e. expressed. Spontaneous behaviour or responses to an environment result in what Sarah Rubidge calls "The functional expressive movement form" – the form of expression or communication we use in our everyday lives.

The fundamental emotions: joy, excitement, grief, fear, anger, contempt, shame, surprise etc., have innate patterns of expressive behaviour which motivate and shape the way we move. Dance and choreography are related to all the fundamental emotions. The dancers/choreographers through their imaginations are involved in expressing and transforming feelings and emotions into an "aesthetic expressive movement form".

In dance, a choreographer may want to communicate that one person's attitude is flirtatious towards another. The movement patterns selected for these moments in the dance are based on the choreographer's understanding of flirtatious behaviour, and through his/her imagination he/she manipulates the movement in such a way that it expresses flirting, although the people who are the dancers are not necessarily flirting with one another. But the audience sees "flirting," knowing that these are not the real behaviour/expressions of the people dancing. As the dancers create these flirtatious forms between one another they too are using their imagination to express, in the form of movement, flirtatious moments. As dancers, our involvement in creating these moments means that we experience a multitude of kinesthetic (bodily) sensations and as a result have a variety of personal feelings, but they are not *expressed* by the *dance movement* for *perception*.

The medium of expression whether of the "functional expressive movement form" or the "aesthetic expressive movement form", is the body and its movement. The body is a person reacting spontaneously to a living environment, or a person responding deliberately to a created environment. The first refers to unconscious behaviour and communication in our everyday lives and the second to conscious creativity in dance.

When dancing is only a behaviour pattern in our everyday life, the expression is that of private and personal feelings of the person dancing, in other words, self-expression, where more often the emphasis is on getting rid of energy. When dancing is art, the expression is that of imagined feelings transformed, through the body and its motion, into an aesthetic form which requires deliberate control of energy.

If in competition dancing "self-expression", sometimes referred to as "personality", is acceptable, then the judges are judging the people dancing, giving personal opinions about the dancers and not making a judgement based on the dancing, the dance itself. We need to stop and think about what it is that is being given credit, what is being valued, what is either good or bad, successful or not, and how is it judged to be so? A stylish dress, a good looking woman, an unusual hairstyle, shapely legs, a "nice" smile? Is there one Latin American image/ideal that the dancers aspire to and contrive to "look like" and that the judges look for?

There is enough evidence that these aspects are considered to be very important. It is also evident that these dancers spend a lot of time, energy and money practising and being coached on their set competition programmes. It becomes clear that this process is the preparation for a performance that has a specific goal. That goal is to win. Dancing to win separates the dancer from the expressive potential of the dance and also from themselves. By that I mean that even the spontaneous joyful participation that is so much a part of social dancing is lost in the effort to win. So what is left? Highly energetic action with some facial expression added for good measure?

Is this dance? Is this self-expression? Is this what judges/audience/dancers call personality? I would like to suggest that those dancers who deliberately search for the expressive potential in their programmes will "feel" self-expressed by this process and will be able to control all aspects of the dance creating an "expression" which has integrity of form.

Imagined Emotion

There is confusion between private emotion and imagined emotion. A simple guideline could be that the context, the environment, dictates this difference. In mundane movement, our ordinary daily behaviour, our movements are expressions of our personal emotions. If we take those exact movements and repeat them on the dance floor they will be the symbolic expression of those emotions not the private emotions of the dancers dancing. But the dancers' imagination will help them to transform the feelings of those private emotions into symbolic expression.

The problem in Latin American dancing is that expression is taught to be something separate, something put on top of the movement, or not taught at all. The reason being that feeling should happen spontaneously during the performance, otherwise it is artificial. This view clearly separates form and content and implies that expression and feeling are different from the actual movement itself. This lack of clarity means that dancers go out on that floor *adding* expression to their steps because it is expected that they should do it spontaneously. So what do we get? A form with a separate expression or an expression which outdoes the form.

The dancer needs to be encouraged to find his/her own way of expressing his/her form which is different from another person's. The dancer should learn to feel that the form can contain only a certain amount of feeling before the mental expression outdoes the physical form. When this overtaxation happens, it becomes "over the top."

Symbolic Expression

In nearly every opera the singers play the role of someone who dies. We do not leave the opera house upset by this "death". We know they get up, go home and do it again tomorrow. We are emotionally touched through the way the singer uses his voice, as the painter uses colour, line and shape, as the dancer uses movement. In Latin, the audience is not excited because the bull is dead or the dancers are happy or in love. We perceive not actual love, happiness or death, but we perceive and share symbolic expression of such emotions.

Susanne K. Langer recognizes that dance consists of expressive gestures of emotion that are not symptomatic, immediately felt emotions, in response to a stimulus. Rather, the gestures are recollected and imagined by the dancer and transformed into forms symbolic of the idea or structure of feeling. In Susanne K. Langer's words: "Everything illusory, and every imagined act (such as a feeling we imagine ourselves to have) which supports the illusion, belongs to the symbolic form: the feeling of the whole work is the "meaning" of the symbol, the reality which the artist has found in the world and of which he wants to give his fellow men a clear conception". (1)

It will not help to create a dramatic Paso Doble by giving the dancers terrible news a few minutes before they enter the dance floor, as Langer states: "It is imagined feeling that governs the dance, not real emotional conditions." According to Langer, expression is not the artist's own actual feelings but what the performer knows about human feeling: "It is a developed metaphor . . . that articulates what is verbally ineffable . . ." (2)

Social Environment

Another confusion in Latin dance is that when the choice is made that the end result on the dance floor must look "social," it is not social anymore because of the change in context. The dancing is not taking place in the authentic social environment, so the function and purpose change. The purpose is to give "social dance" a form in order to share it with the audience and the new context is competition dancing.

The decisions taken by the Latin dancers themselves will dictate whether the expression is their own or created by their movements, so that what is perceived is virtual expression. In other words, if the dancers are concerned with "creating their roles" and creating the partnership that their particular programme suggests, they will be concerned with interpreting the dance movements in order to reveal the meaning of the dance to us, the audience. What we perceive and then endeavour to interpret is the meaning of the dance, not the private or personal feelings of the people who happen to be dancing. The moment the dance is over we immediately engage with the dance couple on another level, as themselves. We may notice by their behaviour as they walk off the floor, that they were pleased with their performance; in this case we notice and read their actual or personal feelings expressed by their behaviour.

This does not mean that during their performance they had no true feelings or thoughts of their own. But the purpose of dancing is not to convey them perceptibly or meaningfully to the audience. If the dancers decide to use their dance programme as a vehicle for self-presentation, an aesthetic environment is not created, so the audience does not make the mistake of searching for meaning but merely enjoys the dancing. In this way they may be impressed by the energy and precise activity of the dancers, while appreciating them as themselves, therefore perceiving the more personal and actual feelings expressed in this activity.

The approach to the dance remains the dancer's choice. But this choice requires a sincere commitment on the part of the dancer if the audience is to appreciate how his particular dancing functions.

The following discussion on aesthetic expression is intended to provide the dancer with a deeper understanding of how dance performance functions and supports an artist's approach to competitive Latin dance.

Aesthetic Expression

In order to understand dance as artistic practice we need to understand that this practice involves an understanding of how the aesthetic functions.

An experience is said to be aesthetic when the object of attention is perceived as valuable for its own sake, and that perception is accompanied by aesthetic emotion. A beautiful sunset, a leaf falling from a tree can be the object of aesthetic emotion and experience. When you intend to have one or to make an "object" for aesthetic appreciation you adopt an aesthetic attitude. But you can also intend to have an aesthetic experience or expect to have one by going to a dance theatre performance, visiting an art gallery or reading a poem. Aesthetic emotion is the knowledge that confirms the attached value to the object and confirms that the aesthetic experience has been had.

Unlike the concrete and accomplished painting or sculpture in a gallery, dance, as a work of art, is always in-the-making. More like music it is only while it is being performed that it can become an object of attention to which value is attached. This is because the medium of dance is the body and its movement, and the body and its movement are the artist dancing.

Virtual Form

For the Latin dancer making an aesthetic choice means that the actual execution of steps is not the focus, but that the concern lies with the movements as a means by which a meaningful "whole" is created. The interaction of the movement structures and interrelationship of the components of the dance medium are inseparable ingredients of that "whole." The dancer might *do* a particular step, but beyond that the manner in which he does it, what precedes and follows, whether he does it towards, away, or passing his partner, the accompanying music rhythm sound, the colour, line, texture of his outfit, his focus etc., all "create" that moment in a particular way, creating the intangible virtual form. The dancer's knowledge of these inseparable ingredients which work together to form the whole is essential if he is to be aware of his control over the dance as it is being *made* in performance. What is done is actual movement, but what is created, is an intangible virtual form. Providing the dancer sustains the "living-through experience" of the dance in its full concreteness, the dance *can* be enjoyed aesthetically by the audience.

To enjoy aesthetically means to exercise perception for its own sake, and not for practical purposes. In the competitive Latin American context it would seem that the expectations of the audience are of a practical nature, i.e. they are concerned with who wins. This, however, does not exclude the possibility of the audience adopting an aesthetic attitude. This is not an "either/or" situation. On the contrary, the adoption of an aesthetic attitude by both dancers and spectators can only serve to enrich the quality of the audience/performer rapport.

Competition dancing can be approached, perceived and experienced aesthetically, but when it is strictly goal-oriented, related to the practical purpose of winning, the dance will remain in the functional realm where movement satisfies a functional need. The question is, whether dance exists in a world other then the mundane practical one. Monroe Beardsley writes: "Because of the highly concentrated or localized attention characteristic of aesthetic experience, it tends to mark itself out from the general stream of experience and stand in memory as a single experience." (1)

It would seem that the above description of aesthetic experience is compatible with how most dancers would like their performances to be received and remembered. While compèring the 1993 Star Latin Competition, I asked the audience during the final round of the Rumba to refrain from applauding and shouting. My intention was to allow for the possibility of the audience to attend to the dance in a different way. In turn, this gave the dancers an opportunity to become involved in what they were doing, how they were doing it, what they were making. The audience-performer rapport changed significantly for the duration of that Rumba. These are the conditions under which theatrical dance functions and the conditions which foster aesthetic experience. This is one example of how competitive Latin dance can be appreciated aesthetically and need not be so far removed from artistic practice.

One of the dangers is to link the notion of aesthetic emotion with other emotional experiences. When dancers or members of the audience are "moved" by the music or overcome with emotion due to their personal relationships with one another, this experience is not to be confused with aesthetic experience. Are you struck by the dancers costume, are you excited about winning, and are your tears of joy an aesthetic experience? These are all examples of functional emotional experiences, emotional personal responses outside the realm of the aesthetic. To feel and sense for the dancer, to perceive for the audience is not to merely receive a message but to participate in an immediate way. This participation is part and parcel of the aesthetic experience and that experience is one that, in its uniqueness, stands out from the ordinary stream of things.

"Beauty" as a Problem

It is a common misapprehension, not only in the Latin dance institution, that "aesthetic" is a nice word for something that is "beautiful."

The term "beautiful" and how differently people use it is problematic. In the Latin dance world, is "beautiful" something we are used to seeing, something we expect to see and accept as beautiful? Do we find a stretched leg and high-heeled shoes more "beautiful" then a bent leg and a bare foot? If so, is this a silent acceptance of other people's concept of "beautiful"? Why are clear shapes in space and erect postures related to classicism seen as more beautiful then African or South-American dance where pure physicality and indulgence in weight, rhythmicality and dynamics take over from preoccupation with forms? Is this strictly true? The whole question of what is beautiful is related to socio-cultural issues and values, a vast area which requires in-depth study.

It often happens that we watch a couple on the dance floor and afterwards exclaim, "They were beautiful." We need not necessarily have had an aesthetic experience. We might have simply noticed things about them, things they did which we have learned are correct and good and attribute value to, calling them "beautiful" because we are prepared to perceive them as such.

Aesthetic Education

The development of aesthetic awareness requires education, and this does not occur in the lesson situation simply through the teacher's criticisms or guidance when new programmes are being created. It involves the inclusion of other forms of art, learning to appreciate how art functions in the form of poetry, theatre, other dance forms and styles, painting, sculpture, music etc. Participating as an audience, as well as taking classes in other dance forms, will enrich perceptions, understanding and aesthetic experience.

In order to develop aesthetic awareness, the Latin dancers' sensitivity toward perceptual, intellectual and emotional experiences needs to be deepened and integrated into their being, before it can become an integral part of their dance. It is my belief that the more Latin dancers understand about this way of participating, the more the audience participation will be heightened.

Abstraction

"Man" and "Woman"

One of the pitfalls/problems in Latin American competitive dancing is the tendency to emphasize the "narrative" element of a couple dancing together. The "male part" tends to become increasingly macho, exceedingly heterosexual. This image is created by the overt gestures in the choreography, the exaggerated facial expression, the exaggerated costumes and by the accompanying clichéd commercial music. The "woman's" part is exaggerated in the same way, presenting an unsubtle image of a stereotyped sexy female.

All too often dancers are taught to be more sexy, feminine, butch, macho, masculine, even words as "high class prostitutes" are used to explain the characterization. I believe that those words are insulting to the dancer as a human being and even suggest that if we are ourselves, we are not man or woman enough. As a dog may walk on his hind legs, but cannot lose his "dogginess", so a dancer, who is a human being, can never lose his "humanness." Because a dancer is a person, he or she can never be wholly abstract. A male person is a man dancing, a female person is a woman dancing. When a man and a woman are dancing together, a statement is already made. Nothing more is necessary to create man and woman, one does not have to "act" like a man or woman as well.

In dealing with this problem the notion of abstraction can be particularly useful to the choreographer and the dancers themselves. They have a joint responsibility. "To abstract is to draw out the essence of the matter. To abstract in art is to separate certain fundamentals from the irrelevant material which surrounds them". (1)

Movement Structures

We can draw out the essence of a moment in a dance by attending to one or two of the movement structures. We are already either a man or a woman, so we can diminish the "acting out" of our "maleness" of "femaleness" and concentrate on the fundamental structure which gives that particular moment its "life" in the dance.

To do this it is essential to understand how the flexible torso movements, the zig-zag parading floor patterns and the alternating impulse/impact rhythms of the Samba are its very essence. They are the fundamentals of the dance and need to be created by the dancer. They do not exist outside of the moving dancer's body. When the dancer changes the emphasis from torso to hips, spending time sinking into transferences of weight, sliding past and circling around his partner, merging impact/impulse rhythms to create a continuity of movement, we no longer see the Samba, but rather a Rumba created by these movements collectively. Devotion to the motion will more economically, more clearly, more accurately, more excitingly, more subtly create the essence of the dance.

About western ballroom dancing Martin confirms "that in dances of this character the curved line is predominant in design. Sometimes this is for the sake of emphasizing the natural curves of the body and sometimes it is to keep the eye of the onlooker constantly returning to the body." (2)

So abstraction in Latin American dancing might be a commitment to twisting actions, changes of weight, staying on the spot, and qualities of weightiness. To add irrelevant extras reinforces stereotyped and behavioural gestures that have nothing to do with the dances.

In Latin this has to do with the degree of abstraction from the subject matter, the male/female relationship. When the emphasis is too much on telling a "story," there is nothing left for the imagination of the spectator. Over-abstracting might create a feeling of being too far removed from the dancers, giving the dance a cooler impression with the emphasis on design, form, or space. A male/female relationship in Latin dance should sustain the illusion and leave something to the spectator's imagination. It contains a semblance of reality that we can identify but not so clearly presented that we can name it.

Choreographic Implications

Choreographers who have, as dance teachers, the most influence on the dancer's performance need to understand abstraction as an aspect of the creative act.

When an idea is to represent a cape, one first has to learn to lift the abstracted qualities, the lines shapes and rhythms from the source of motivation. Secondly, the abstracted qualities need to be removed from their every day setting. In the Paso-Doble the "cape" is not in the bull-fight arena and is not a "real" cape. It is symbolized through the female dancer, who remains female and is not in the arena. She creates the illusion of a cape. Thirdly, the choreographer has to organize those lines, shapes and rhythms into a form that holds the original concept as an abstraction. When not abstracted, i.e. when the woman tries to "represent" the cape as literally as possible, it can become comical rather than representational. Although this example is obvious, the same applies in more subtle representations like the flirting behaviour of the male/female and the creation of the characterization of each dance.

The dance should sustain an illusion and not endeavour to represent the idea literally. The illusion contains and is created by the abstracted elements manifest in the shape and form of a moving human being, and therefore embodies feeling which is symbolic.

Form and Content

Because of the preoccupation with the body and technique, dancers can easily fall prey to the misapprehension that form is physical shaping. Often "steps" or "figures" are taught through demonstration and copying. Thus physical structuring is the experience of form for the dancer, and physical shaping in space is the form perceived most readily by competition audiences and judges alike. They deal with content as completely separate from form, as smiles and gestures added to it. The purpose of this discussion is to prompt the reader to think further about form in relation to content, form as the "shape of the content".

Even shape as the physical form is something I prefer to create from "within." Stretch the leg on "count 2" put your arm outwards on "count 4", keep your head up etc. – information given this way sounds like the leg or arm does not belong to the dancer. It is not a leg, but YOU that is moving. It is *your* leg, your arm. It is the feeling elicited from stretching, the sensation of lengthening, the awareness of giving attention to and consciously sending out energy from within, which gives the stretching its quality and gives it its shape.

"Shaping up" the body in the form of "pumping iron" or toning the body can be done through aerobic exercise, weight lifting etc., but also through exercises which consider the human being as a whole. Shiatsu, Yoga, Tai Chi are not only physical exercises but take into account the emotional, spiritual aspects of the human being "shaping up", not only the physical body, but shaping the inside into an outer manifestation. Rodin, the sculptor, when asked how to become a sculptor answered "Oh, that is easy, you take a big stone and take away what you don't need." In relation to shaping he did not say, "Oh it is easy, you take a stone and put the ears and nose on top." No, he shaped the inside to an outer manifestation. So in a sense, the shape of the physical form comes from within. It is shaping the content: the content is the human being, the body is its form.

The shape of the physical form is a single element of the whole. In dance, however, it is not about single elements but about how the ingredients form a structure and how that structure creates the "umbrella form", that which holds the individual ingredients together in organic unity. It is the dynamic energy of the interrelationship of the content which comes alive and creates a form which is the shaping of the content in dance.

The following quotes will support this concept. Susanne K. Langer: "The illusion, which constitutes a work of art, is not a mere arrangement of given materials in an aesthetically pleasing pattern; it is what results from the arrangements, and is literally something that the artist makes." (1)

John Martin: "Organic form is the relationship of elements by which a self-determined identity is created with an inherent function emanating from the interoperations of its constituents, each of which is indispensably related to the whole." (2)

Material Coming to Life

It is clear from these quotes that form in dance is quite specific because of the nature of dance material itself. The medium of dance is both dancer (physicality) and movement in all its complex arrangement of structures, body, action, space, dynamics, relationships. Together with the score, the space, the lighting, the costumes, the props, dance performance finds its form and its content. Then the framework that holds that performance or allows it to function, theatre, competition floor, created space, further forms the dance and creates its content. For example, the exuberance and vitality of the Samba are its content and its form, while the sensuality and twisting and weight tranferences of the Rumba are its content and its form simultaneously. All the ingredients come to "life" in such a way that one can not exist without the other. They belong together, they are inseparable in that form.

Form and content cannot be separated. As you cannot be separated from your leg, the dance cannot be separated from its content. In Latin American dance, form and content are often separated. There is a tendency to add "the nose, the ears to the stone" rather than to discover it in the making, shaping it from within. The emphasis on creating an "image" in Latin dance for example, a dynamic sexkitten, a sophisticated romantic, an animalistic undulating look, a gypsy look, often results in this image being acted out and become something of a decoration put on the dancer instead of an embodiment of the dance. Just as the "image" needs to be formed within the dancer in order to become the dance, you cannot just add a stretch here, a rhythm there and a new and different costume tomorrow. Find the changes within first, as content, and then the shape, the umbrella form will be created. Like an umbrella, the form covers only what can "fit under it." Accessories, unnecessary ingredients, should be taken away, so that the content fits the form and the form fits the content.

In dance practice this clear conception can easily be lost as choreographers set out to "put steps together", to create a programme, or as dancers engage in repetitive practice of their "steps". In most dance practice/styles/disciplines form is most often thought of as technique and content as the expression. This leads to a separation of technique from expression. Dancers learn their steps, then try to add the expression, mostly facial, while they do the steps. Subsequent chapters in this book address this problem specifically while advocating an approach which confirms Ben Shahn's notion that "form is the shape of content," and that technique cannot be separated from expression.

Chapter 4

Dance Education

Learning and Unlearning

So far I have advocated approaching competitive Latin American dance as an artistic performance. I have outlined how this approach requires an aesthetic attitude on the part of the dancer. But what about the role of the teacher and the process which will encourage, allow and foster this? The process will require not only dance training but dance education. These two aspects need not be separated in practice.

The concept of education is enormous, but here I will discuss only some aspects of education that have influenced my approach to Latin dance. The main focus will be on the learner/teacher relationship, and not an examination of the educational institution. My approach has also been determined by the principles of choreology, holistic practices, performance experience and teaching experience. The following quote (from Al Huang) introduces some shared and important issues: "As a movement teacher . . . I find the most difficult thing is an *unlearning* process that we have to go through. . . . Unless you come with emptiness and openness I can give you nothing. We need that kind of ignorance, in learning and dealing with things every day." (1)

To be "empty and open" in the learning situation does not mean that one gives over the responsibility for learning to the teacher. On the contrary, it means that the student opens up to the different phases of learning which ensures what in educational terms is known as "autonomy of the individual" (the learner) and the aquisition of "open skills". The opposite approach is referred to as "indoctrination" and mostly results in the learner aquiring "closed skills".

Cognition and Skill

When one sets oneself up to teach dance, the primary element taught is skill. Learners pass through fairly distinct phases in the learning process, so that the final phase may be easily recognized when achieved. Where all kinds of dance training take place, the cognitive phase is most common. Training seems to be solely concerned with the mastering of the most effective way of *doing* something. Once that has been determined, repetitive practice of routines and programmes takes over. It is not uncommon that "practice nights" are spent repeating programmes again and again. It is also not uncommon for further instructions to be given during each lesson. This is not only common in the Latin dance world. It is common where the acquisition of technique (skill) is considered important. In other words, the training consists of the teacher giving instructions and the learners (dancers) trying to find a way of carrying them out.

There is more to dance training than this. The associative and autonomous phases need to be included. That is where dance education begins, and becomes a part of the training process. It is clear from the table on page 70 that once the autonomous phase is reached, individual autonomy is possible and "open skills" are said to be acquired. An open skill is one where the dancers can not only make choices for themselves, but can make them on the spot in unpredictable situations, for example, in dance competitions.

A closed skill usually remains inconsistent in performance because if the conditions are changed, the instructions upon which the performance is based no longer apply. The dancer is lost. R.S. Peters gives a pertinent example which has important implications for the consideration of educating the dancer. Spartan soldiers were morally and militarily trained. They knew how to fight and they knew what was right or wrong according to code. In other words they had closed skills. But they were neither morally nor militarily educated. Failure to grasp the underlying principles of their code led to the unintelligent application of rules, the inability to make exceptions when confronted with unusual situations. (2) In other words, they needed open skill (called "intelligence") to deal with unusual situations.

It can be generally agreed that the acquisition of "closed skills" leaves a dancer in a situation where he must rely on the judgements, comments or instructions of others, because the basic principles which hold that skill together are not understood by the dancer himself. Dancers have to make their own decisions, choices and judgements based on their own understanding of those principles which hold a skill together, and based on the knowledge of the body which using that skill provides. This way – and this way only – dancing becomes "authentic".

A teacher who approaches teaching with openness allows for the same openness on the part of the learner. This enables new discoveries by both parties and the mutually growing development of the expertise of both teachers and learners. The openness also encourages trust, vulnerability and the development of understanding through discovery. It also supports a fundamental aim of education, the autonomy of the individual. Peter Brinson outlines the importance of gaining knowledge through discovery and first-hand experience rather than through instruction and explanation alone: "What a child hears, he forgets; what he sees he remembers; but what he does, he understands." (4)

Hearing and seeing are not enough. The new ideas must become part of the "organic system". How many times has the dedicated teacher heard a student exclaim "Oh, now I see! That's what you meant last week!" A week later the idea has begun to make sense to the student. Not until it becomes a part of him does it take on real meaning. (5) Tai-Chi also reiterates this way of gaining knowledge and understanding: "By moving very slowly you have time to be aware of all the subtle details of your movement and your relationship to your surroundings . . . You reach a level of speed that is like slow-motion, in which everything is just happening. You slow it down to the point that you are fully involved in the process of each moment as it happens." (6)

You simply have to work with the movement until you discover it in your own body. "I can show you how I do it, and I can give you some ideas about how it can be done, but you have to discover it for yourself as you do it!" (7)

It often happens that there may be nothing obviously wrong with what you are doing, but you just don't have it yet. The suggestion here is that it is in the process of doing that you come to know and understand. In dance, doing involves, thinking feeling and creating, and it involves the dancer as a person on more than a physical level. Our intellectual, intuitive, physical and emotional selves should be involved, if we are to make a "significant utterance" in the dance medium. Most dancers practise their dances to music, repeating them in the same way. My suggestion here is to turn off the music, repeat your dance in a variety of ways to discover more about it and about yourself as a part of it. This way the dancers need not "follow" the music, but discover the "music" within the movements of their bodies.

Wisdom of the Body

From the wisdom of our own body we learn pure movement, uncluttered with outside knowledge. You cannot learn to dance from ideas and instructions alone. Knowledge from inside coupled and balanced with knowledge from outside is required for the sensitive aquisition of dance skill. (8)

The teacher's responsibility then, is to create an environment within this development and involvement may occur. But all too often teachers feel that, unless they give information or manipulate the dancers' bodies in some way, they are not really "giving" and "teaching". When first attempting to teach dance, people often take on the role and method of those who taught them, and indeed this is encouraged and even admired in some instances. Dancers who teach often try to teach by showing what they themselves can do, instead of leading others to their own thresholds, their own unique development. The educator Ryle remarks (1967): "the role of the teacher is to show the pupils the ropes. It is up to the pupils to climb them." He adds that "teachers must realize that their pupils may be able to climb faster and higher then they can."

In a sense the teacher of a Latin dance couple plays a "role" in the dancers' development. The nature of the relationship should be a professional one, i.e. one in which the teacher's philosophy about dance is shared with the dancers in a way that leads to their independence and perhaps finally to the need to detach themselves as learners.

Autonomy

When pupils reach the stage where they no longer *need* the teacher, this is surely the ultimate compliment. The autonomy of the individual has been achieved. It is common that the relationship between teacher and pupil becomes very personal, but this kind of relationship allows for a blurring of the roles, and in many cases leads to an emotional dependence on the teacher and to an inability to develop outside of that relationship. When more distance is encouraged between teachers and pupils, a closer professional relationship seems to emerge. With this distance, it appears that what is taught "becomes" the dancers' rather than the dancers taking something on loan from the teacher.

As a teacher, I have discovered that teaching for my own enlightenment, out of an awareness of my own body, is fully satisfying for me and the learner, and it provides for both discovery and individual development as well as understanding of the movement itself. By providing education together with training, the teacher gives learners the power to make their own decisions, to find their own way, while still receiving the necessary guidance and challenge, encouraging a simultaneous consolidation of skill and an understanding of that skill.

Three Steps Forward

So far, this discussion has mentioned certain major aspects which contribute to the achievement of "being educated" in dance, the mastery of skill, the acquisition of knowledge and the understanding of principles. Richard A. Schmidt identifies the three above mentioned distinct stages or phases which learners appear to pass through as they practise a skill. The first and cognitive phase is where the major gains occur in terms of "what to do." This stage involves retaining good strategies. The second and associative phase is when more subtle adjustments can be made in "how" the skill is performed. The third or autonomous phase is reached when the performer gives the impression that he or she is performing without having to "pay attention to" the actions. This stage has the benefit of allowing the person to process information from other aspects of the task, such as the form or style of a movement in dance. (9)

Collectively, these aspects involve processes which are incompatible with what is known as indoctrination, a prevailing attitude within many genres and styles of dance training. Indoctrination is a hazard where mastery of skill is required. A skill is, by its very nature, not something that can be immediately learned and retained for all time. Constant practice is absolutely essential. Skills, by definition, are difficult to master. Practice needs supervision. There is no escape from practising the specific type of performance which has to be mastered. The general term for this type of learning process is training. A teacher may provide an incentive for this kind of learning, but the learning never takes place without the practice.

I.	**Cognitive Phase**
Teacher	gives instructions: which pattern of actions, which steps
Learner	new to the task: understands what is to be done, tries out strategies, keeps some and dispenses with others
Gains	largest and most noticeable in this phase
Time	hours to days
Performance	usually inconsistent

II.	**Associative Phase**
Teacher	gives information on how to do steps/pattern particular
Learner	by now, the most effective manner of execution determined; more subtle adjustments as to how a skill is performed are learned
Gains	improvements more gradual; changes are small but significant
Time	days to weeks
Performance	becomes more consistent and more effective

III.	**Autonomous Phase**
Teacher	information is reduced
Learner	becomes automatically more efficient, can possess more information from other aspects of the task
Gains	high level of skill; audience's impression is that the performer need not pay attention to actions
Time	months to years
Performance	becomes concerned with higher aspects of the task; egg-form of the dance.

Al Huang writes: "Do you really believe that you can become a great artist simply through practice, practice, practice? I think not. I think there must also be a lot of inner growth and vitality along with discipline. An athlete may require a trainer to keep him on a schedule, keep him going. But without an inner sense of growth, a trainer can beat you to death without getting you anywhere." In dance training, the perfect delivery of a known vocabulary is encouraged through repeated practice. Consequently, dance training's repetitive practice tends to encourage the acquisition of closed skills which do not further the autonomy of the individual.

The Problem of Demonstration and Imitation

There is "a sense in which we really do not know what we think about anything until we have had to state it explicitly and defend it." (10) If this process is encouraged, eventually the learner internalizes the questioner and critical thought develops. This process encourages that ability and the tendency to formulate principles and thus clarify one's understanding of them. Conversation is the opportunity to contribute distinctively to a common world. This is not possible without knowledge, understanding, objectivity and sensitivity to others. It is "a valuable learning situation of an informal sort." (11) Indoctrination demands formality, acceptance, and discipline *for its own sake*, thus leaving the educational experience open to question.

Just as practice without thought is a useless activity so is copying the movements of others. Exploration, improvisation, explanation is all-important because the final result belongs to the dancer, not the teacher.

An observer might say, "Why go through all that? Could you not show the back extension and then let the student do it?" Yes you could, but the result would be different. The student can imitate and arrive at the same general position, but the movement is not the same. In the method described above the learner is deeply absorbed and highly conscious of the action. He gets "inside" the movement, so to speak. He understands the internal relationship and develolps a kinesthetic awareness of the action. (12)

In the words of R.S. Peters: "Dance should be experienced as an expressive activity, not as an imitative endeavor, because if one is to create dances he must be able to state himself." (13)

Personally, the less I demonstrate the more the pupils have to think, feel, do, make for themselves. They have to become more creative and the end result, no matter what the level of skill, is more sincere.

When dancers become teachers, the temptation to use demonstration as the common mode of instruction is strong. But as Alma M. Hawkins writes: "As a teacher, the individual must shift his attention from a personal involvement in dance to the task of helping students relate to dance. In this reversal of roles the focus shifts from fulfillment of self to the release and fulfillment of others. If the teacher is dedicated to the task, the adjustment can take place easily and a new kind of self-fulfillment will result from helping others to achieve." (14)

Not only is it necessary to redefine their role, but teachers are also required to understand that all their students do not have the same motivation: "The teacher must recognize that the student responds to the dance situation as a whole person, as a totality. He comes with certain feelings that may be identified as eagerness, fear or indifference. Along with his feelings about dance, he has feelings about himself and about his life. His response to the particular learning situation in dance is affected by all of his feelings. When he enters the dance studio, he does so as a whole person. He does not bring any special parts of himself and leave the other parts outside the studio." (15)

To summarize, in Hawkins' words, a positive learning environment needs to be established as follows:

1. Focus on dance as a creative experience.
2. Experience dance as a whole activity.
3. Clarify and refine the parts in relation to the whole.
4. Expand the frame of reference for dance.
5. Develop critical awareness and the ability to make aesthetic judgements.
6. Keep the individual as the central concern.
7. Evaluate in terms of individual growth. (16)

Conclusion

It is clear from this discussion that the concept of education in relation to dance brings up many issues, but the single most important issue here is the empirical view of knowledge, which argues that knowledge derived through our senses, through our direct experience of the world, is valid knowledge. Knowledge is created by the learner through direct involvement in solving problems and making sense of experiences. The rationalist view of knowledge is based on the claim that data received through our senses are unreliable, while intellectual knowledge is superior. In such cases, learners are not perceived as *creators of knowledge*, but *receivers* of already existing knowledge. In education today we find elements of both traditions.

This chapter, I hope, will encourage teachers and learners alike to clarify for themselves the processes, the stages, the what, the how of educating and training in dance so that experiences and goals become compatible and appropriate for our specific practice.

Creativity

There is a common conception that by simply kicking convention in the teeth one is being creative. Before you can oppose anything, before you can break rules, you have to know what it is you are opposing, what it is you are violating, and how. It must be based on technical competence. Before you change the rules, you have to know the discipline of the medium, the principles defining conformity. In other words, to "deform" you have to know the form.

Exploration

During the process of creating, the dancer/choreographer needs to explore his sensory world, his cognitive world and his affective world. From this search unique expression emerges in the form of a dance. This creativity requires openness to new experiences. (1)

Can creativity be taught? Of what value is it to the Latin teacher, choreographer or dancer? Carl Rogers writes that psychological safety and freedom are two basic conditions needed for creativity. (2) A.M. Hawkins endorses this by saying that psychological safety evolves from a working situation in which the emphasis is an acceptance and understanding of the individual, with a minimum of external evaluation. In the dance situation this means that the student needs to feel that the teacher accepts him and his creative ability. He needs to know that his creative effort will be respected even when the results do not reach the desired goal: "Just as other students display their paintings and read their poems, the dancer should show his choreography. It is through performing and sharing his work that he is able to overcome his feeling of isolation and increase a sense of belonging. As the student becomes convinced about the sincerity and respect that surrounds him and his work, he will find it possible to relax and be more daring, as well as to work without making excuses or putting up defenses." (3)

Creativity can thus be nurtured or fostered in the individual by the situations or conditions in which the teacher/choreographer and dancer/student relationship functions. It is easier to turn to standardized goals, means and ends, rather than to face the insecurity of finding one's own solutions and way. Some teachers are unsure of freedom and relate it to permissiveness, preferring an orderliness that can be controlled. But real creativity is contradictory to conformity, i.e. restrictions, order and control, and is frightening because it involves personal responsibility, self-education and courage from all participants in the process, i.e. teachers and pupils, choreographer, dancers.

If the autonomous development of the individual as artist is the goal, then creativity is not only a valuable tool but an essential part of the educational process in dance practice.

In Latin dance practice creativity is often confined to the teacher/choreographer who creates the programmes for the dancers. But the dancers can so easily participate in this creative process if the teacher allows them to explore the medium and to share their discovery of something which becomes the dance. When choreography emerges from the dancer's active creative participation, the dancers are more creatively involved on the competition floor as well. They will be more aware of their participation as an act of creativity, rather then simply performing a given programme detached from themselves. This involvement is often termed interpretation.

Choreography

In Latin dance the activity of creating a dance is loosely called "choreography". The emphasis is on "putting together" a "programme", which involves putting combinations of (basic) steps (belonging to the Rumba, Cha-cha-cha, or Samba technique and which present the style of each dance) into a sequence.

It is important to acknowledge that theatrical dance functions in different ways. It appears that the theatrical approach to creativity/choreography has much to offer the creative process in Latin dance. The following suggestions and points discussed are presented out of a concern to increase the awareness of choreography as a creative, educative, and training process, for teachers and dancers who are active in competitive Latin dance.

Generally, the choreographic ideas are stimulated by such things as experience with a given style, inspiration from music, historical information, parallel or contrasting styles, imagination, instinct or technical knowledge. Once the ideas of the choreographer have made their impact on the movement, the dancer's commitment to the material must be made with a full awareness of what the dance is about, otherwise the dance becomes an automatic routine which the audience perceives as monotonous. In other words, the choreographer's intentions must be known and respected by the dancers if that "something" which the dance is "about, related to, concerned with" is to be perceived by the audience. The translation of the choreographic ideas into movement by both the choreographer and the dancers is a unique and special process. It is a relationship which results in that special quality that makes observers want to get involved. They become integrated in the dancework during its performance.

One of the criteria of successful choreography is that it has a structure to it, a form that progresses through time, a chronological beginning and end. Using the linguistic model, the notion of structure is clearly demonstrated. A group of single letters form a word, words form phrases, phrases form sentences, and sentences texts. The choice of letters, words etc. and their organization conveys "something". In dance, isolated and single movements are linked to elements, form cells which together create a motif, motifs form phrases with sections, and sections organized in sequence form the whole. (1)

It is not enough to think only of structuring, finding the right words to say something; we have to be concerned as well with the intonation which can change the meaning. Hamlet's monologue can be "killed" just as much by monotony as by overemphasizing; empty words can be "blown up" by rhetoric and dramatic highlights can be rendered in different styles (emotional, as ironic understatement etc.). In other words, "content" and "intonation" have to match each other. In dance, the dancer has the final say; his "intonation" on the "content" can only be witnessed in the presentation.

It is not to be suggested here that the choreographer should be preoccupied with intellectual and analytical structuring during the creative process, but that is important to recognize that "structuring" is part of the manipulation of movement material. So if a "programme" is devised by just adding more and more movement as you go along, the emerging structure is less likely to enhance the content of the programme. Whereas if a choreographer consciously structures the content, the "dance" will emerge as a whole, related and "formed up".

Essentially, structure cannot be separated from content and, to a certain extent, structure is the content. For example, in a Latin Rumba, when the woman does a "Curl" she may look down, turn away from her partner and then face him. She could also do a "Curl" by changing the structure, in other words by changing the order, first facing her partner, turning away and then looking down. If you experiment with this you can see that the order, the structure is the content, i.e. whatever "meaning" arises, it is created by the sequence of steps.

As mentioned before, the act of structuring is not arbitrary. It is said that a "good" phrase of movement grows out of the preceding one. Following the principle of affinities, bending actions lead to stretching, overbalancing leads to falling or travelling, twisting leads to turning. But to create interest, going against the affinities creates unpredictable phrasing, e.g. twisting into travelling into bending into overbalance.

No matter what you choose, a basic principle in phrasing remains: the notion of "preparation/action/recovery". Or on a larger scale, a clear beginning, a climax and an end. The first has to do with the control of energy while executing certain movements and the second to do with the dynamic level of the work. The first relates to the dancer's control, the second to the audience's perception, but both are decided upon by the choreographer. They are part of the choreographer's structuring of the dance.

Phrasing

A dance phrase is like a musical phrase, it has to do with the structuring of speed, duration and accents. In Latin dance, the relationship between phrasing of the music and of the movement is integral to the style, but this relationship can sometimes serve to limit the creativity of the movement structure. If the music dictates the creation of the phrases of movement, an automatically predictable stream of aural and visual structures ensues and, though it may be easy on the eye and ear, interest can rarely be sustained because the repetitious rhythms (structures) supersede any choreographic intention.

The relationship between music and movement in Latin can be complementary. Generally this is the accepted idea; the "dance music" is made visible through the "dancer's movement", but this conception is simplistic and boring if applied constantly and automatically. While you remain committed to the basic three steps to a four beat bar in the Rumba for instance, choreographically you can let it go in order to pick it up again. Or take the Paso Doble highlight, where there is a clear stop in the music. Does that mean there should be a stop in the movement? Not necessarily, as long as you are aware of how to relate a movement to this momentary "stop" in the music. However, if you are unaware of what you are creating through this relationship, the audience won't see it either and it will look like you have made a mistake.

Variety is desirable but must also be appropriate. In the Samba, where the musical phrases are of equal length, predictability is often a problem and movement becomes boring. To have all phrases choreographed with the same shape, dynamic level and duration creates monotony. A point of rest in a dance is not a dull thing, as most competitors feel. It is significant in relation to the structure. In dance, pauses can give importance to the past or bring attention to the future or hold attention for that moment, the present.

The important thing to understand about phrasing is that by consciously structuring the movement in relation to the structure of the music, you are in effect creating an organic unity. This creation of unity of a whole is also sharpened by the choreographer's attention to the larger sections of the dance through which it progresses. These larger sections can be held together by carefully structured transitions so that the spectator is carried along and the illusion sustained. Each transition acts as a bridge that binds together the sections and sustains the continuity of the dance. But again, the exact way in which the parts are related must be determined by the subject matter of the dance.

All too often in our style-bound dance form, choreography can end up looking like a whole lot of steps strung together. Attention to the dynamic level affords solutions, resolutions, and connections. These enhance the sense of progressive development. Without this the dance may well be structured but not unified. A unified whole is created, not through variety, but by the interrelation of the larger and smaller parts (cells/phrases/sections). Similar phrases with similar subject matter can create monotony, while different movements out of character (in other words: not related at all) can be disturbing and indeed do not serve the characterization.

Basic and Complex Patterns

In the contemporary dance world countless theories and approaches to choreography are shared and put forward. The following selections might be helpful to those who are interested in "choreographing" dances for competition as opposed to making dance programmes.

Repetition is a notion that many choreographers approach in different ways. It is a common choreographic device because it serves to create the organic unity discussed above, and it serves to assert the particular character of the dance in a variety of ways, while underlining the subject matter. There is, of course, boredom of repetition. On the other hand, there is enjoyment of repetition: the state "house dancers" get in when repeated sounds fit the repeated movements. The enjoyment of repetition of turning and travelling in the Viennese Waltz, for example, or even that of the long distance runner. In Latin dance repetition is seldom used as a device. In fact, there is a greater fear of repetition because dancers constantly try to outdo the ones before, and be newer, bigger, faster, building on each moment to continue creating an impact. The competitors are tempted to follow one climax with another. It is not unlikely that a dance will start with a forceful, strong, sudden grabbing and throwing of each other on the first two bars of the music, only to grab each other in the same way again and again.

Repetition in the form of "a-b-a" or "a-b-b-b-a" or "a-b-a-c-d-a" helps to ensure a certain audience response. "A" refers to the opening phrase or figure, "b" could refer to a basic step, "c" to the second phrase, "d" the third phrase. Using the device of repetition, no more completely new material would be added. But as the dance progresses from "a" (the opening statement), to "b" (a contrasting statement), building to an inevitable return to the opening theme, there is a sense of satisfaction, a recognition of a cycle at work but with no kind of predictability, because the return to "a" can be different from the initial "a" – richer, smaller, slower, simpler perhaps. Predictability is negative when the result is boredom, but positive when the final "sense of inevitability" arises. Without repetition, new materials are continually added, which means that there is little or no relationship between the beginning, middle and end. Those movements are merely arbitrary parts in a linear unrelated progression of steps, and endings have no significance to the whole. It might be argued that the Latin dancer's programmes are not presented in a way which includes the expectation that the audience will watch the "programme" from beginning to end. However, the dancers experience and know their programmes as a "whole", something that has a beginning, middle and end even though they may not get to perform "the end" on the dance floor.

Judges are never able to see the whole work of a dance couple while judging because they have to look at all of the couples' work. This is probably one of the reasons why choreography, in the sense that it has just been discussed, is frequently not logically structured. Through the desire to impress (in the few seconds that judges may give to them) rather then express, we often see programmes full of highlights, tricks, gimmicks all the way through. This is very difficult for dancers to sustain in terms of energy and interest. I believe that a logical progression in the choreography would be more interesting and comfortable for both the dancers and the audience, and that this in turn would have its impact on the judges too. At the moment, most dancers are just using their "programme" as a vehicle to compete, whereas choreography properly understood would present the dance itself.

Theme, Variation and "Story"

The idea of theme and variation used in musical compositional structure is another choreographic device that could be useful to the Latin choreographer. The final result of a theme and variation is a sequence consisting of a phrase of movement repeated a number of times with different shadings. The theme is therefore the basic structure. The variation is the theme repeated in the same sequential arrangement but with different dynamic resonance, with a different character or expression.

Quite often, the narrative provides the organizing principle for the creative structuring. In the narrative collage, care must be taken that the "story" does not overtake the structuring but that it informs the structure and that the structure is the narrative. The choreographer has to find movement that is revealing of inner nature of emotional states. Care must be taken that the "story-telling", i.e. the movement selection is not literal but that the manipulation of movement both shapes and narrates the dance. To say it simply: Do not *act the story out* by frantically trying to supply them with "expressive" gestures, pantomime and being "dramatic". If the audience wants to see only a story they go to the theatre and watch a play.

The danger of any formal structuring is that creating the form becomes more important than the artistic intention. It is the end product that counts, that is perceived, and not the principles or devices used, that count or need to be recognized by the audience. A dance must look as if it has been "born" rather than crafted, which, realistically speaking, in nine out of ten performances is just not the case.

Give and Take

The mutual task shared by choreographer and the dancers is an important one. The choreographer may have wonderful ideas, but the dancers may not be able to dance them. Obviously, the choreographer's expectations should be realistic but challenging for the dancers. Dancers in the theatrical world have a variety of classes for specific practices, a technique class for training, developing the dance instrument (their bodies); the improvisation class for exploring and finding their own movement and expression; the choreography class for the development of imaginative forming of movement; theory classes for developing an understanding of human movement in different contexts etc. The Latin dancers' experience of dance is normally through their sole engagement with their programme. As a result, the choreographer in the Latin world is also the teacher, the one who trains the dancers and educates them.

A teacher has to set his expectations at the level of the dancers' ability when choreographing a dance for them. But how does the teacher/choreographer challenge the dancers so that they can improve? You can create a dance in such a way that it challenges specific abilities, so development of these abilities is ensured. Extra fragments of material can be given over and above their structured dance. These can be worked on, providing an opportunity for training and development. It might be possible to add them to the choreographed dance through a restructuring process.

Improvisation

If the Latin teacher/choreographer takes the responsibility of training and educating, there are specific approaches to creativity which will reinforce and ensure the training and education of the dancers. One of these approaches is improvisation. Working through improvisation directly involves the dancers in the creative process. Sometimes misunderstanding arises from this method; dancers are under the impression that they are now doing the choreography. While improvisation uses the dancers' instinctive movements and responses to situations, to suggestions and to each other, it also increases awareness of the material during the process of "forming up" the dance and brings them closer to it. In other words, the final product is something they believe in as part of themselves and not something that has been simply "put on them" by the choreographer. The final decisions are made by the choreographer, as to what to put where, i.e. as to the structure and the artistic statement as a whole.

One possibility is to let the dancers improvise on a theme in the hope that they are stimulated to create movement which can be repeated, developed and put into the work. This way, the choreographer comes with the theme and the dancers' responses to the theme are studied and utilized. In including the dancers' creative ability and individual choices of movement they become personally, physically and emotionally more involved in the dance. Because the resulting movement is not intellectually predetermined and imposed on the bodies of the dancers, a spontaneous quality is introduced to the process and to the performance, giving integrity to the work.

The improvisation process works two ways; it is a way of "finding" movement material and it develops the individual style of the dancer. Another point is that, when stimulated creatively, innovative solutions are more likely to be found where the intellect is sometimes "stuck". Improvisation encourages originality as it develops, especially when it is task oriented. It develops sensitivity towards the movement itself. A task may be to emphasize different body parts or to give different and changing dynamic resonance to moments. This use of improvisation provides not only a choreographic device but a training and educational process.

During the performance of the choreographed statement, the dancers' contribution is vital and the only manifestation there is. The choreographer may visualize ideas, concepts, structures, and imagine how the work will be manifested, but finally he depends entirely on the understanding, technical skill and physical make-up of the dancers. So the more they are involved in the creative process, the closer the relationship they have to the dance and the closer they will be to the artistic integrity of the piece.

Appropriate Response

An important task for the choreographer is to ensure that the evolving material not only communicates or holds the idea/intention, but also that it conforms to the style. What is the audience going to perceive? Do you have the most appropriate "ingredients" arranged in an order to convey the intention? To use an analogy, have you put pepper into the spaghetti for pepper's sake or have you put just enough to sharpen the taste? The exact amount might not be noticed but the difference will be in the taste!

Within the structure of the dance there is a beginning, there is development and there is a resolution. The climax is sensed as the high point that leads to the resolution. The dance starts, goes somewhere, and arrives, giving a sense of completeness.

Sometimes a lack of structure is a result of the dancers' approach to the material, sometimes a result of how the material has been choreographed. All too frequently in Latin we see a dance made up of totally different phrases of movement throughout the programme. Too much variety destroys unity. A dance consisting of totally different phrases following one another is ineffective because, as Hanya Holm writes, "you can create movement that is technically correct but not yet choreography."

In the Latin world there seems to be a tendency to think that the more complicated the material, the "better" the dance. The real problem is that if you are not technically proficient enough to perform something simple, you try to cover up that deficiency by doing something complicated in order to arrive at a sense of achievement. In this case, the choreographer is ignored as an artist and the dancers use their complicated routine to present themselves. I suggest that the choreographer needs to be aware of the dancers' attitudes to performance so that he can choreograph appropriately. For example, a choreographer can create a dance, *using* Louis van Amstel and Julie Fryer as dancers, or create a dance in order to *present* Louis van Amstel and Julie Fryer themselves. The choreographer needs to be clear about the aim and purpose of each choreographed piece.

Choreographic Exploration

Another approach to choreography is through exploration, a more structured process compared with the process of improvisation. It involves a more conscious search for movements within a limited framework. The aim of this process is to push both dancers and choreographers beyond their more habitual way of moving, the external motivation developing internal motivation.

The final process, the organization of movement found through improvisation or exploration, involves the selection of fragments and ordering of them into an organic whole, which will give significance to each dance. This is the concern of the specific choreographer. One of the problems in Latin dance, with regard to the notion of dance as a "whole", is that when dancers go from teacher to teacher with their "choreographed programme" and one teacher changes a bit here, the other a bit there and so on, you are left with a completely different whole, a different dance, which perhaps lacks integrity, inasmuch as the original structuring was "the dance".

Assessing the dance is also part of the final process of choreography. This involves checking if what you "perceive" is what you actually intended to make. Are you still in contact with the whole rather than its parts? Are there movements where you are lost? Why? The success of the dance is dependent on the economic use of material. Ideally, the form should be so organized that nothing can be added and nothing taken away. Every movement and quality must belong and contribute to the internal structure. Simplicity is the essence. All superficial, peripheral, unrelated material must be rejected. Taking a step back from the work also protects style. A choreographer must take care that the material used conforms to the genre of Latin American dance by virtue of its characterictic selection. The choreographer's own personal style also needs to be easily identified thus supporting his distinctive contribution to the institution. The individual style of the dancers, especially if improvisation and exploration is used, will support the distinctiveness, the merging of the dancer's and choreographer's style to form a stylistic whole, a sensitive synthesis, an organic form.

Authentically all dances were improvisational in character. The male and female meet on a social occasion and dance together making the dance as they go. Basic "moves" are manipulated and basic rhythms keep them together. It is possible to make a "programme" which is made up of basic figures and easy lines, in order to manipulate them spontaneously on the competition dance-floor. Or partly devise a programme and have moments in which you can improvise and then go back to the set choreography. This is common practice in Standard dancing. But a competition event is not a social occasion, it is a performance. We do not meet our partner for the first time on that occasion. We have been practising for this event. Real presentation of the dance presupposes real knowledge of the dance.

A set choreography does not mean a set expression, we do not know the exact tempo or melody we will be performing. We do not know what atmosphere the event will create. Therefore, it can never be the same. The choreography (*what* we do) can be the same, but the dynamics (*how* we do it) can be improvisational. Generally, we change the dynamics and small body parts while performing. Where we touch each other, for example, gives emphasis to different body parts and changes the feeling (dynamics) of a step.

If I am going to see Swan Lake ten times, I expect to see swans every time, not elephants because they're tired of being swans. Of course Swan Lake is not only about swans but through their floating arms and feathery gestures we perceive the metaphor. I am not bored when I have to view the same couples doing their same dances for five rounds, provided they present their *dance* each time. But when they only present themselves I am bored very quickly, for they just cannot sustain presenting themselves five times nor create an impact or feel new excitement each time.

Choreography and Programme

The following table draws some interesting parallels between the *presentation of the dance* I have termed choreography and the *presentation of oneself*, called here a dance programme.

	Choreography	**Programme**
Intention:	to create the dance	to display the self
Rhythm:	including movement rhythm	timing to steps and counts
Phrasing:	relation to movement	to music only
Climax:	built up to	constant
Subject matter:	being male/female	acting male/female
Structure:	beginning, middle end	linear progression of figures
Presents:	the dance	technique and effects
Ending:	creating an end	stopping

Chapter 5

Non-Verbal Communication

The 17th century provided an environment out of which two distinct parallel developments in dance emerged, theatrical dance and social dance. On the one hand the French masters of dance elaborated the steps and, as master of ceremonies, insisted on formal behaviour and technical precision. This emphasis led to the development of classical theatrical dance, commonly understood today as classical ballet dancing. Aristocratic youth looked elsewhere for entertainment and it is suggested that this constant search by youth for entertainment is the historical root of both popular dance and social dance. (1)

Today, popular dance and social dance share a similar style because of their common roots. The participants are, or portray, a heterosexual couple who through their bodily communication relate to one another, create a specific relationship. Their bodily movements belong to our nonverbal communication system, which plays a central part in human social behaviour.

In contrast, the standardization of technique, which has historically distinguished social dance from popular dance and which has set up a traditional approach to the teaching and learning of its vocabulary, has become the primary stylistic feature of the institution of Latin American dance today. This preoccupation with steps and technique tends to divorce Latin from its social historical roots and to ignore the bodily communication inherent in its vocabulary. The dance critic John Martin writes: "Any theory of dance that attempts to make use of the body as an instrument of pure design is doomed to failure, for the body is of all possible instruments the least removable from the associations of experience . . . It is totally out of the bounds of possibility for a man to raise his hand and kick his foot or bend his torso without implying something in the movement. If he tries to do so, he merely says in effect to the spectator, I am now actually thrusting or pulling, or fleeing or reaching or rejecting, but excuse it please, for what I want you to see is only the line and balance of forms as elements in design." (1)

What he is saying is that human movement means something, whether it is dance movement or not. Dancers and audiences respond to the body language of their times. The steps, the figures, the programmes Latin dancers employ are not perceived as a Hockey Stick, Spot Turn, Allemana etc. by the audience, nor are they perceived as lines in space. Instead, the gaze or focus of the dancers on one another, their posture and particular body movement required to produce "the step", their bodily contact, their spatial relationship as well as their appearance all contribute to what is "virtually" perceived at that moment. Although the dancers may be totally engaged in performing the steps and figures, inherent in the resulting movements is the virtual expression of the dance i.e. the "meaning".

Conscious and Subconsious Body Language

One might argue that if the expression, the meaning is inherent in the movements, why bother to be aware of it? Can't it just speak for itself while we get on with the steps? Yes, you can do that, but your performance will remain something over which you have little control. You will not be aware of what is being perceived by your spectators. I am not suggesting that you think about the inherent expressiveness of your movements during your performance, but rather that reflection in practice educates an awareness of how movement is perceived, "read" and communicated, and this awareness makes for a felt, controlled, projected performance.

As Martin writes, it is not possible for a human being to make any movement without implying something. The human body cannot *not* communicate. A woman facing a man but averting her gaze while he focuses on her directly makes a statement before a single step is performed. It appears as though our preoccupation with steps and technique has resulted in dancers treating these as the *text* of the dance and ignoring the *subtext*, i.e. what is inherently there by virtue of the fact that dancers are not arms, legs and feet, but human beings moving with all the implied associations of human movement.

In 1991, I danced a duet to Mahler's 5th Symphony with Peter Townsend, as part of a lecture demonstration at the World Congress in Blackpool. The intention was to demonstrate how a change in the ingredients of the dance, i.e. the music and the dancers, affected the entire expression/meaning. While we were occupied with dynamic changes and spatial forms, the audience perceived a relationship between two *men* and some were disturbed by this to the extent that they perceived nothing else. The point here is that no matter how well controlled our steps, our partnering, no matter how clear the choreography, we were two men looking, touching, gesturing, partnering one another and this was the essential expression. The steps made no difference at all.

Nonverbal communication, eye movements and facial expressions, postures and gestures "that we all use more or less consciously and more or less effectively – can enhance or diminish every form of social interaction." (2)

An awareness of these bodily changes inherent in the Latin vocabulary/technique and their expressive potential will lead to their conscious use and will enhance the effective communication of "the dance". It therefore seems reasonable to want to understand the nonverbal communication within human social behaviour and to do this we need to untangle the system.

In his book *Bodily Communication* Michael Argyle identifies a number of main nonverbal signals. The following have significance for Latin dancers:

- facial expression
- gaze
- gestures and other bodily movement
- posture
- bodily contact
- spatial behaviour
- clothes and other aspects of appearance. (3)

Approach and Withdrawal

The following discussion will examine how an awareness and conscious use of some of Argyle's main nonverbal signals might be useful for the Latin dancer. But before examining these individually it is helpful to identify, in general terms, the nature of the communicative relationship which a Latin dance presents. We have already established that the "players" are male and female and that the choreography often presents this relationship as sensual in motivation. The relationship is an intimate one, which is primarily expressed by the following signals and channels: proximity, level of gaze, degree of self-disclosure and other cues for affinity. Flirting is one of the most repeated behavioural ingredients of social dance. Flirting behaviour has been interpreted by behavioural scientists as the result of the conflict between approach and avoidance. A study of Latin dance programmes reveals that when the approach-avoidance equilibrium is maintained, the programme is more succesfully flirtatious.

It is understood that in situations of intimacy, people are attracted and repelled. If one person likes another, the forces of approach will be stronger and the forces of avoidance weaker. It follows that if a person comes "too close", this will arouse stronger avoidance forces than approach forces, so that the other will be disturbed and back away. If a move or signal is interpreted as a pleasant event (for example friendly), there will be reciprocity, whereas if it is interpreted as unpleasant (e.g. embarrassing), there will be withdrawal. In this way the avoidance-approach equilibrium, in other words "flirting", is being maintained.

Now we will examine how the intimacy, sensuality and flirting nature of this relationship is maintained both by the structure of the choreography and the dancers' interpretation of "the dance."

In his study of interpersonal attitudes, Argyle identifies two dimensions of attitudes toward others.

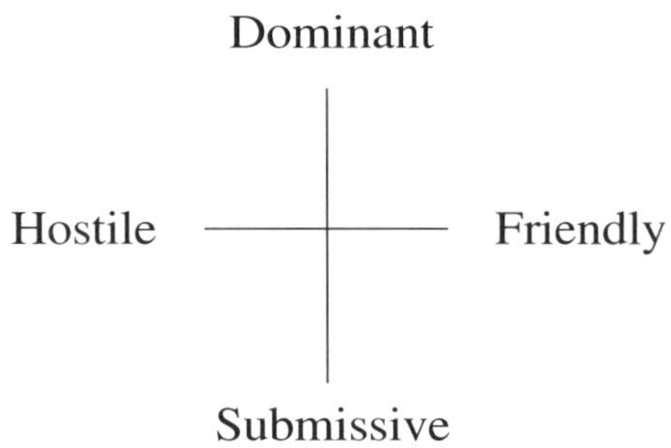

This model explains the most important dimensions of attitudes toward other people, how much they are liked or disliked (affinity) and how much intimacy is desired. The main signals for affinity are:

Proximity:	closer, forward leaning if seated
Orientation:	more direct, but side by side for some situations
Gaze:	more intense gaze and mutual gaze
Facial expression:	more smiling
Gestures:	head-nods, lively movements
Posture:	open with arms stretched towards other, arms on hips or folded
Touch:	more touch in an appropriate manner

Looking at the above table, it is quite evident that the Latin dance vocabulary itself is rooted in these signals, and it becomes clear how many times, in various ways, a dance programme requires these signals.

Argyle's signals for dominance are as follows:

Spatial Position:	height, e.g. on a raised platform or standing (though sitting is a sign of status on some formal occasions), facing a group, taking up more space
Gaze:	in an established hierarchy, less gaze, but relatively more looking while talking; when trying to establish dominance, more gaze and staring other down
Face:	non-smiling, frowning, face with mature adult features
Touch:	asymmetrical touching of other
Gestures:	pointing at other, or his property
Posture:	full height, hands on hips, expand chest, relaxation in an established hierarchy. (5)

Vocabulary and Grammar

An analysis of several couples' competitive performances reveals that several of these signals of dominance and affinity are used by the dancers, especially the male dancer. The question here is whether they are appropriate to the intimate flirting relationship of Latin dance. A closer look at sexual attitudes and their signals suggests that the approach signals of flirtatious communication and signals for dominant behaviour might easily be confused or mixed up. An approach signal can be both dominant and friendly, but constantly used dominant signals will characterize aggression and not the flirtatious qualities necessary for the Rumba. Equally, there seems to be some confusion between the signals for submission and those used for avoidance in the flirting conflict.

When two people are sexually attracted to one another this is communicated by a particular set of bodily signals. These include signals for affinity with the addition of the following special signals:

Gaze:	a high level of mutual gaze, pupil dilation
Touch:	in appropriate places and ways, depending on the situation, e.g. kiss, embrace, hold hands
Posture:	"courtship readiness" expressed by an erect posture, increased muscle tone, pulling in the stomach, arms open or stretched towards other
Gesture:	woman preen themselves by, adjustments to hair and clothes
Appearance:	individuals likely to enhance their appearance, attention to clothes, hair, and skin; accentuation of the apparent size of eyes and of the sexual organs. (6)

It is clear that these signals are part and parcel of the Latin dance programme. Argyle and others even go so far as to suggest a universal structural sequence followed by two people of the opposite sex, as intimacy between them increases. These are also pertinent where dance/programme structure is concerned:

1.	Courtship readiness:	high arousal, bodily alertness, grooming.
2.	Position for courtship:	face to face or side by side.
3.	Actions of appeal or invitation:	gaze-holding, protruding breasts, rolling pelvis, hand on hips etc. (7)

Awareness of the bodily communication system, its channels and signals illuminates the Latin vocabulary and technique, in that it reveals the sociocultural environment in which the movements originate and which influences and suggests their meaning. Ignorance of this system can lead to a misinterpretation of the vocabulary, a misrepresentation of the intimate flirtatious nature of the male/female relationship, an over-indulgence in the presentation of the self and the over-reliance on facial expression, which serves to diminish the interaction between the dance partners themselves and between the dancers and their audience.

The Treatment of "Male" and "Female" in Latin American Dancing

It is not enough for the dancer to simply know about Argyle's techniques and signals. To imbue those recognizable signals with nuances, impulses and inner stirrings, the actual structures of the moments in movement need to be understood, so that exciting and appropriate choices can be felt, controlled and projected. It is not the gazing at your partner which is going to create the moment, but *where* you look, *how long* you look. Is it *mutual* gaze, is it *awareness* gaze. Do you move your gaze, let it pass over him, or penetrate through him? The way in which you attend to the movement structures of the particular signal will imbue your dance with meaning.

Are we preoccupied with the stereotyped heterosexuality of the Latin dance couple? If you seriously step back and watch what is coming at you from the competition dance floor, it is possible that you might think so and feel that the whole preoccupation has led to a destruction of the possibilities and subtleties of this relationship. The immediate context of Latin dance is the competition dance floor. There, all the strands of the medium are already working before the dancers prepare to do a single movement. The audience is gathered on all sides, socializing, eating, drinking, expecting entertainment and results. The lighting and decoration create a glittering arena of expectation. The music moves from romantic to disco at exaggerated levels of volume. The dancers are clad in colourful revealing costumes, generally exaggerating the female and male sexuality and sensuality in often unsubtle ways. All this is a statement in itself. The dancers do not have to contribute to the exaggeration by making faces, and giving *all* their energy *all* the time. But this is a common occurance and indeed perpetuates exaggeration as an aspect of the Latin dance institution.

I would venture to say that, generally, Latin American dance practice reflects a misunderstandig of how the male/female dance partnership functions and,, equally, its mismanagement on the dance floor. It is not only the dancers who are guilty, but also those who write about and comment on dance competitors. A glance through any of our dance magazines will reveal reporting that refers to the personal identities of dancers and very seldom explicitly to the dancing.

The question is, whether it is more desirable, especially for a professional dancer, to be remembered for their personal appearance or for their dancing. The appeal and possibility of the latter is confirmed by the following comment on the Burns/Fairweather partnership: "They, more than any of the other couples, show the personality of the dance fused with their own indomitable personalities rather than solely their own individual identities." (1)

Judith Lynn Hanna, anthropologist, remarks that dance transforms everyday movement for its material and that male-female stereotypic movements, learned early in life, are part of these everyday movements, therefore part of dance material. Signifiers of social inequality appear in contrasts, in posture, precedence, elevation, movement quality and touch. She offers the following interpretation: "In lateral opposition the right side is associated with strength, justice, moral integrity and beauty. Assymetry indicates imbalance in status, whereas symmetry or reciprocal behaviour suggests affiliation and equal status. Verticality expresses deference and authority. The upper to top height is high status, . . . the lower, becoming horizontal in bowing and prostrating, connotes inferior status. . . . Higher status people touch lower status people more than vice versa. Touch may convey power, dominance, aggression, comfort, love and sexual arousal." (2)

The above signifiers of inequality appear throughout Latin dance "programmes" and indeed support and reveal male-female stereotypic behaviour. The point being made is that the male-female roles are already there in the structures of the dance and need to be understood rather than exaggerated.

The following table makes use of Hanna's findings but uses categories that are pertinent to a structural study of Latin dance movement. (3)

Stereotypic Non-verbal Gender Specific Behaviour

	Male	Female
Body	wide in stance, thighs separated, pelvis slightly rolled back (walk on flat shoe)	narrow stance, thighs together, anterior roll on pelvis (walk in high heels)
Action	large sweeping gestures, arms and hand one unit wrist, forearm	smaller gestures, articulation of fingers,
Space	controls greater territory, uses more of personal kinesphere, tends towards verticality, initiates directional changes	yields to other's space, uses less of personal kinesphere, tends towards horizontality, reacts to such changes
Dynamics	does not wait, begins actions, direct gaze, holds gaze over time, less flow in movement, high energy with sudden, strong, direct, expansive energy	"woman-in-waiting" responds to actions, flexible gaze, looks but averts gaze, more flow in movement lower energy with sustained, lighter, less direct, expansive and contractive energy
Relation- ship	uses a lot of focus, prolonged approaches closely	uses less focus and for shorter periods, approaches other women closely but is usually approached by men first
	touch often, encompass woman, touch themselves less	touch less touch themselves more

Appear-ance	clothing allows more movement and relaxed body comportment	clothing (skirt + heels) constricts movement and constrains body comportment
Face	uses less, smiles less	uses more, smiles more (friendly signal)
	less likely to return smile when smiled at (dominant hostile signal)	likely to return smile when smiled at

Old Time Roles

Finally, this chapter cannot conclude before admonishing the fact that the portrayal of women in Latin dance continues to ignore woman's sociopolitical reality today. To some, indeed many people, the portrayal of women as mere objects of sexual desire, thrown around by men, treated as men's pleasure is wholly distasteful today. It still strikes me as incredible that during the final heat of a competition the "announcer" can ask the audience to show its appreciation of a female competitor's looks (never a male's) by applauding accordingly when their number is called. The portrayal of man also needs rethinking. Stereotypic behaviour is only a cliché today. There are many different expressions of maleness which do not relate to aggression, power and dominance. To preserve any self-respect, the Latin dance institution would do well to examine aspects of its functions which are insulting to male and female competitors and spectators alike.

The Comparative Nature of Movement

The language of movement has deep structures and surface structures which, in their complex relationships, influence meaning. Those principles which organize these structures in a particular way at a given moment in a particular context, need to be identified and understood if the inherent expressiveness of the movement forms are to be apprehended.

Of particular interest to Latin dance is the insight into one of these organizing principles offered by Warren Lamb and Elizabeth Watson (*Body Code – The Meaning of Movement*). The theory of posture-gesture-merging (PGM) is presented as an organizing principle. The theory illuminates the continuous and integrated nature of the function of posture and gesture. This has particular importance for the dancer.

Consider whether any gesture on its own can ever give us reliable information. Like all behavioural scientists, Lamb and Watson assume that to examine gesture you have to do so within the context in which it occurs. For them, this context, this environment, is the whole-person-in-action, creating an entire sequence of rhythmic movement where gestures and postures relate in a particular way. Within this flow of movement a small gesture such as a wink or raised eyebrow might be highly significant, but its significance is related to the whole, and can only be interpreted in that context. In other words, the smallest twitch of an eyebrow is only significant in relation to the body posture in which it takes place.

Posture and Gesture

Lamb also highlights the distinction between posture and gesture by adopting the phrases, "making" a gesture and "having" a posture. But he cautions that there is no such thing as a fixed posture; "a posture is always posturing". (1)

Thus we arrive at the notion of a range of posturing or posture patterning. By releasing the idea of posture as something static, the meaning of postural expression can more easily be located and sought for in bodily movement. In other words, a "posture profile expresses itself in posturing or movement". (2)

Gestures are generally made by the head and limbs, especially the arms and hands, and generally accompany speech. They replicate or mimic the form of some idea the speaker is trying to depict in his verbalization. Gestures can be referential, demonstrative, tactile, facial or emphatic.

Language can be deceptive, but there is a school of thought that believes that movement never lies. Lamb suggests that much gestural movement can be contrived and that, in general, we get a truer reading from posture. In other words, we can more consciously manipulate the gestures that we "make" than contrive the posturing that we "have".

When the body is in motion, as when dancing, one action must lead to another and this action-sequence may be confined to the part of the body where the action originated, or it may spread to take in other parts as well. (3) The latter refers to Lamb's theory of PGM where the movement might originate as a posture and merge into gesture or vice versa. In such cases the movement has a continuity and consistency flowing throughout all the involved parts of the body. For example, when hand to arm to shoulder to head and rest of body is one instrument in total expression.

The nature of movement is apparently co-operative. (4) Actions which take no account of the whole body are both felt and seen to be a source of discomfort and cannot be maintained for any length of time. The essential quality of PGM is flow of movement, which means segregation is not possible. Where there is segregation of posture from gesture there is no PGM. Lamb goes so far as to say that there is a link between merging and spontaneity and segregation and contrivance. Experiments have shown that a high degree of segregration is found in people who are trying to create a false impression, when people are not telling the truth, or are in awkward situations, trying to give the impression of ease. A high degree of merging is found in confident spontaneous behaviour.

He suggests that where particular movement skills are required, their mastery depends on the achievement of PGM. He highlights the approaches of coaches, trainers, teachers of movement skills by examining the practice of starting out with required gestures or with a required stance. But these can only be starting points. There is also a process of postural adjustment to the required gestures, which needs to be learned. If the teacher is not a movement specialist, Lamb suspects that the real movement skill will be left out of the training altogether. He concludes that the more a person's movements are performed with PGM, the more their behaviour and movement skills will be observed as spontaneous or apparently so, characteristic and sincere.

The Whole Truth is the Truth of Wholeness

In this way, and through this learning process, the learners/dancers become involved in a holistic way, without separation of mind and body. Warren Lamb writes, "When body and mind function in an integrated fashion, we can observe posture and gesture merging (PGM) where action is consistent throughout the body as a whole." When PGM is performed, both mover and spectator report a feeling of ease, naturalness and involvement.

In Latin and Standard dancing there is a tendency to over-use gesture and separate it from posture. For example, when the lady's head in Standard dancing is isolated from her body alignment, it becomes a gesture. When an arm or hip action in Latin becomes separated from the posture, it becomes a gesture. A gesture in itself is not wrong, but if one gesture follows the other or is constantly held, it becomes artificial.

Latin dances often use gestures to create a specific effect. A woman places her hand on her hip to suggest, a man raises an eyebrow to reinforce his macho image. What needs to be examined is the posture on which that raised eyebrow is supported. Try it out yourself. Stand with legs apart, look down on a woman and raise the eyebrow. Step away from the woman look away and raise the eyebrow. Experiment and you will soon see that on its own, raising the eyebrow means nothing and is expressive when merged and felt as one expression with posture. Indeed at times these separated and repeated gestures can look comical and awkward. When we see dancing which looks natural it will mean that there is posture/gesture merging.

Chapter 6

MOVEMENT

The Intrinsic Structures of Movement Action

Rudolf Laban's (1879-1958) observations and classifications of human movement have influenced a wide variety of practices. Through his invention of a system of movement and dance notation he created a contemporary theory of movement and dance. The discipline of choreology (Laban Centre of Movement and Dance, London) embraces the theory and the practice of Laban's main concepts of human movement. One of the significant aspects of his work is the classification of movement, which provides for a systematic analysis or synthesis of movement structures. Choreology defines the intrinsic structures of movement as follows: the body, its actions, the space, dynamic qualities and relationships.

By presenting a structural view of the body and its movement, it is hoped that the reader will eventually be able to determine and define those structures which are inherent in Latin American dance technique. This approach is possible because the following information is not style-bound and can be used to illuminate the content of any human movement activity. Knowledge of these structures is significant to the dancer because it enables him to commit himself to them so that they may be actualized in performance.

Body

The organization of the body may be visualized in a variety of ways: medical, anatomical, pictorial, kinesiological, erotic, psychological, etc. (1)

Here we will look at the body structurally. The human body, i.e. the dancer's body, has an organization, a structure. The head, torso and limbs are arranged in a particular way, the joints and surfaces of the body link these parts to one another and provide the body with a schematically organized three-dimensional shape. The dancer can draw the audience's eye to whatever aspect of his body he decides upon. It must be remembered that the whole body from top to toe is always active in dance whether in motion or in stillness.

One movement can be danced in a variety of ways when one is aware of the body's organization and structure, of the smaller parts of the body, of which body parts lead a movement, initiate a movement, of where tension is held in the body, which parts are focused on. Knowing these different aspects, we can bring different body units to the audience's attention. A particular and conscious clustering of body units can evoke dynamics, design the space, realize relationships and organize actions.

It can be seen that, in itself, the dancer's body is a grouping of units able to dance congruently, in opposition or independently or as one harmonic whole. (2) Without this awareness, the dancer's intention lacks clarity in performance because commitment to body structures is uncontrolled or even unknown. The body could be seen as the foundation, the ground, the source, the volcano of utterance; the dancer gives his own layer of meaning to the dance through his body's utterance. (3)

Action

In a structural approach to dance the use of the term "action" is quite specific: "Actions are not set movements, but categories of movements, structural units. Actions are dancing structures, not verbal structures. They have no exact names, they have symbols." (4)

Units of actions:

Movement takes place, change occurs, a happening or activity is unspecified.

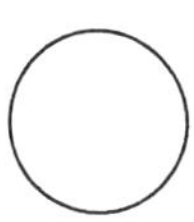

No movement takes place, no change, holding still, pausing, retaining a situation, a tension, an expression.

Travelling, locomotion; maybe running, walking, crawling, rolling, sliding.

Jumping, elevation, take off, landing; maybe change, leaping, sissonne, from feet to hands.

Turning, rotating, revolving around; maybe spinning, fouetté, rolling, turning to face a new direction.

Twisting, turning but one end holding still, parts rotating; maybe twists in the torso, turning out legs, rotating arms.

Transferring the weight, supporting, balancing; maybe stepping, kneeling, lying, handstand.

Gesturing, not transferring the weight, not stepping; maybe nodding, inclining, port de bras, rondé de jambe.

Bending, curling in, contracting, closing, shrinking; maybe crouching, making a fist, retiring, closing into a knot.

Stretching, extending, growing, lengthening, elongating; maybe reaching out, extending the leg, opening a fist, stretching the spine

Overbalancing, falling, moving beyond the supporting leg; maybe tombé.

Inclining, moving to another situation from one joint, not bending or stretching but leaning.

An awareness of the concept of action, and a knowledge of these categories, gives one access to the body and its movements for furthering exploration of the dance medium. Clear observation of these structures of action apparent in and particular to a specific technique opens up movement possibilities for the choreographers' use and the dancers' interpretation, giving a wider range and more conscious choice. In relation to the body, actions can take place in the body as a whole or in body fragments, or in joints or body surfaces, i.e. you can turn your head or turn the body led by the turn of the head, led by the back of the head or by the chin. Each action then becomes quite distinct and unique when led by selected body surfaces, and this awareness and commitment is what turns an everyday movement/ action into a meaningful created dance movement.

A Note on the "Action" of Stillness

Quite often the notion and experience of stillness in the context of motion is considered to be without action. But, of course, holding motion still, arresting it, is not a passive act and requires a degree of strength and muscular control for it to be both experienced and perceived. In dance, stillness is a very important action, not only enhancing clear beginnings and endings but important for the following: a degree of stillness is required in a moment of suspension; the moment between the end of a swing and before the end of another one; or in the hesitation or pause which punctuates and controls phrasing. This is a feeling of hovering in space, of defying gravity. An attempt to preserve the sensation of continued motion in a held position is also an action of stillness. It is recognizable in the extending gesture which has the feeling and appearance of going on into space, a feeling created by the bodily tension and distant focus of the eyes.

Stillness can be experienced as the striking of a pose like vogue, but when stillness is the result of a movement being stopped, the position will then seem to be expressive as opposed to contrived and artificial. The beginning of the Paso Doble often looks like a muscular "frozen picture". However, when the energy of the body is working consciously in opposition, the stillness will be powerful, i.e. full of life, i.e. an action, a kind of movement.

Space

Space is the dancer's context or environment, an "empty void until the dancer fills it with meaning. She enters into it and turns it into a place of expectation, a landscape. She transforms it." (5)

There are several ways to view space besides the above, which refers generally to the dance area, the shared space. But beyond that, each person/dancer inhabits his or her own personal space, a living breathing space with boundaries, created physically, psychologically, socially, culturally. Within this sphere, within this personal space or kinesphere, a centre is to be found.

This sphere can be brought to life by the dancer dancing, "filling it, piecing it, shaping it, encompassing it, disturbing it and breathing it". (6) An increased awareness of this personal space means the dancer becomes acquainted with it. Within it structures are organized, and the dancer can inhabit it in a fully enlarged or in a diminished sense.

Like all habitations, this sphere has dictinct and differentiated areas or places all related to the structure of the body. The layers above and below, the places in front and behind, to the left and right, create the middle layer. As these places are related to body structure, so are they intimately related to certain spatial actions. Rising and reaching takes the body upwards towards the layer above; sinking, lowering, collapsing to the the layer below; expanding and closing actions occur between the body centre and the side areas of the sphere; and advancing and retreating actions use the space in front and behind the body. The body structure and the idea of locations present the body in its three dimensions. Locations above and below and the body structure from head to foot create the vertical dimension. The symmetry of the body, together with the locations left and right of the body, create the horizontal dimension. The locations in front of and behind the body, together with the front and back surfaces of the body, and the ability of the limbs to move in those directions, create the sagittal dimension.

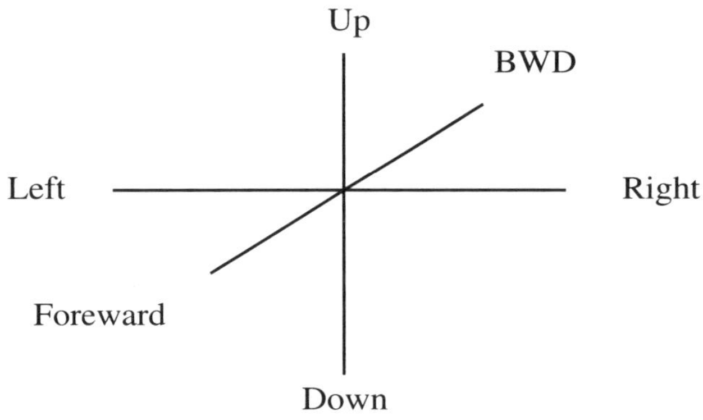

The cross identifies the primary dimensions of the body and the primary directions of its movement. But the body's movement is not confined to these directions. It is helpful for dancers to understand their existence and to depart from them. For example, movement that occurs in the vertical and horizontal dimensions simultaneously can be described as functioning in the "door plane", while movement occurring in the horizontal and sagittal dimensions functions in the "table plane". A combination of vertical and sagittal dimensions creates movement which functions in the "wheel plane". An awareness of the planes can assist dancers in giving clear directional shape to their movement and distinguish them from other movements in other planes.

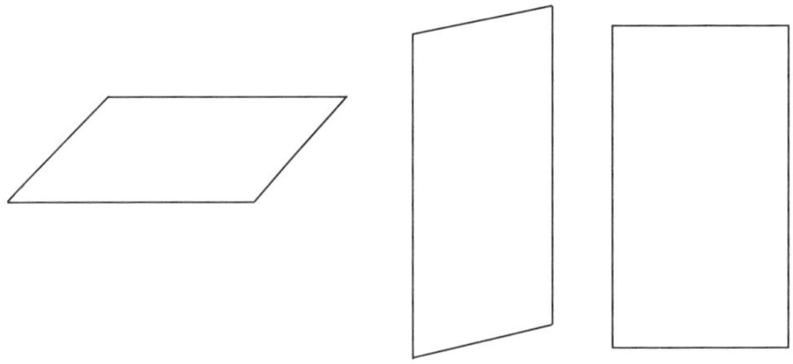

Table Plane **Wheel Plane** **Door Plane**

While the former approaches to space are linked with the body itself, space has its own structures. Spatial structures are seen in dancers' bodies. Spatial structures are mixtures of the following: shapes, sizes, extensions and distances, directions, locations.

Of the above, one of the most useful theories for the dancer is that which analyse the ways in which shapes are conveyed in space in dance. The only units of shape which can exist in space created by the body and its motion, are straight or curved lines. Valerie Preston-Dunlop puts forward a theory based on that fact and suggests four manners of materialization of these straight or curved shapes. (7) The first is body design and is most commonly used. When conveying shape through body design, the dancer becomes aware of surfaces of the body, its textures, sensing the sculptural form and creating it for perception. In this way, the space is taken into the shape and the space outside is ignored.

The second way of conveying shape is through what Preston-Dunlop refers to as spatial progression. Often, movement of a part of the body traces a path through space, and it is the shape of this path that is predominantly perceived and not the shape of the part tracing the path. Sometimes the lines created by the body itself are conveyed out of the body into the space and thus we have the third way of conveying space which is spatial projection. This creates a feeling of ongoing, never-ending distance and often requires using the eyes, the focus, to extend the shape beyond the body and its kinesphere. When a line or band in space is conveyed across the void by the physicality and dynamics of two poles, this fourth way is called spatial tension. This fills the space with vibrancy, shaping the space for perception.

Floor patterns and aerial patterns are conveyed in some of the above ways in different circumstances. Like all information in this chapter, movement does not occur in the way it is written. The four manners of materialization occur in complex sequential and simultaneous clusters, in different parts of the body in a mixture of straight and curved shapes. Clusters are given significance by the nature of their relationships. The following table presents the symbols used to explicate this theory.

Manner of Materialization	*Straight Shape*	*Curved Shape*
1. Body Design		
2. Spatial Progression		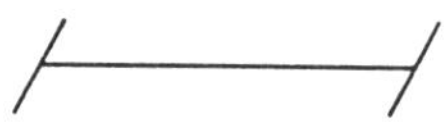
3. Spatial Tension		
4. Spatial Projection		

Dynamics

Dynamics refers to how the movement is performed. Through dance the dancer experiences movement which expresses emotions, moods and states of being. These are revealed mainly through the movement's dynamics. In the dance situation the dancer should be in control of the movement which creates these moods, while in real life the moods often take control of the person.

Laban recognized that the dynamics of movement are created by particular combinations of four motion factors which he classified as *flow, weight, time* and *space*. He came to the conclusion that the dancer's attitude to these motion factors could be either a fighting or an indulging one. When dancers are moving with particular awareness of one of these factors, it is recognized that the other factors are present as well. For example, if we are concentrating on time, then flow, weight and space qualities are present but perhaps not dominant.

Weight

The attitude to the motion factor *weight* is revealed by the degree of force shown in the movement. Maximum resistance to weight produces strong powerful movement, while decreasing this resistance will produce lightness. Decreasing resistance even further will produce increasing heaviness. Standard dancing generally aims to defy gravity, while Latin generally gives into it, but too much of one or the other will create an imbalance in our movement. The weight factor is concerned with the continual fight against gravity to maintain the upright position, without which gravity would take over and weightiness would occur. But you can increase the pressure of weight by getting behind it, pushing it, producing a forceful strong quality or, if you withold, withdraw that pressure, you can produce a quality of lightness.

It is important that a dancer learns to sense his own body weight before he can actually change its quality. Cecily Dell, shares some thoughts on weight which will help develop this weight awareness and sense. She writes about the centre of weight or centre of gravity referring to that part of the body most involved in initiating shifts of weight and generally activating and supporting the body weight. This centre is situated in the pelvis. She also says there is a centre of lightness or levity. (8) This term is used to refer to the upper trunk and more specifically, the sternum. Activation in this area with support from the centre of gravity, provides optimum conditions for lightness. This minimal tension, sufficient to hold the skeletal structure poised, creates the sensation of lightness and weightlessness.

Time

The time motion factor is revealed either by a degree of leisure or a degree of haste. The concept of time discussed here has nothing to do with the pulse or timing or structure of music but rather with timing of movement itself.

All dances, phrases of dances or dance movements have a duration, a period of time during which something occurs. The length or duration of a phrase will be determined by the organization of the series of time elements within it. Mostly when practising, but even when performing, dancers count the musical beat value to find out how long a movement takes in relation to the musical beat. This is all well and good initially, but beyond that the sensing of movement duration has to occur to give the movement/music relationship a character of its own.

Another notion of time includes that of the speed of motion. The contrasting qualities of speed are sudden and sustained or accelerating and decelerating. Creating these qualities requires varying attitudes towards the urgency of an action. An effort may be made to speed up the action or to delay the action. Fighting against or resisting time gives a sudden quality to movement, whereas indulging in time results in sustained slower movements. Sudden movements create feelings of momentariness, a bursting all over before it begins. It is the arrival that matters in contrast, a feeling of endlessness, lingering, awareness of the passage of time is created by sustained movements.

A commitment to suddenness has a feeling of urgency coupled with a sharp desire to reach the end of the movement. If continued, it is exhausting both to do and to watch. Real sustainment has a feeling of being caught up in an unending stream of time. The movement is leisurely, as the dancer lingers over each stage, unwilling to give it up. A balanced sense of time results in the ability to keep abreast of things, neither rushing onto the next step nor letting things get so far ahead of one that panic ensues. An informed attitude and a commitment to the time motion factor, allows the dancer to control the perception of time, to create an illusion of time. With both sustained and sudden qualities, images of past, present and future can be created.

Flow

Flow refers to the control of energy in the body and connects one movement to another. Energy is built up through increased muscular activity, through changes or through control of breath. In everyday life, we intuitively know how much energy to use for a particular action, but in dance that becomes more difficult as we need to become aware of that intuitive knowledge.

Free flowing movements mostly originate in the centre of the body and travel outwards, e.g. from shoulder to elbow to wrist to hand, or from hip joint to knee and foot. Inwardly contracting movements have a natural affinity with bound qualities and extending movements have a natural affinity with qualities of free flow.

Energy is difficult to define. If you feel it, it can give you power, not brute strength, but essential potential power within, to control and create. Whenever you send out energy you have to get it back again. Laban's notion of the alternation of scattering and gathering movements explains the function of energy. The human body is always in a more or less "energized" state. When we describe movement, we must understand that in the human body the engine is always running. This is particularly important for understanding the "opposite" or extreme qualities in the flow factor, the free and bound qualitites.

It is not really accurate to think of the polarities of motion as being extremes in the flow of tension, either bound or free. There is a whole range in "bound" and in "free" and also between those two. It is a matter of "intensity", a degree of concentration in the production of the qualities. There is always energy, you may change it, but the body is always responding to both inner and outer stimuli, like the accelerator of a car, providing a constant stream of urges to move. As Preston-Dunlop puts it: "You cannot produce energy, make an energetic move or muster your energy, if you do not have a capacity for tension in your body ready for use." (9)

As you watch a person dancing, you may notice that he holds or restricts the flow of movement, or that he gives in to the moment and goes with the flow of movement. This restriction is "bound." The going with the movement, which comes across free and easy is "free". It is wrong to think that free flow is better then bound flow. There are no good or bad qualities in effort, there are appropriate and inappropriate uses of qualities.

Energy, when bound, is always within the body, and when free, it can be extended beyond the limitations of the physical self, like an illusory extension of the self in space. This very illusive intangible quality is what gives life to movement and also the motivation to feel the action. Energy is like the electricity of movement.

The output of energy is directly related to the motivation and the strength of the emotional stimulus. Tension and release refers to the depletion of the initial period of energy output and the concluding phase of relaxation or rest. The flow of energy is like blood circulation or like unconscious breathing. When controlled this way energy can really save a dancer. When energy is internally stored or blocked, tension builds up and movement ceases.

Space and its Direction

The motion factor space is attended to by the manner in which the movement evolves in space, varying from direct paths to indirect, flexible meandering paths.

An indulgent use of space results in a plasticity of bodily action. The movement will either be expansive and fill the space about the body, or fold flexibly in the space. Either way, the movement will have a definite relation to the body centre, originating there and involving the whole body. In such moments the eyes will also probably have an inward focus. A fighting attitude to space results in an economic use of space in a definite single area about the body. The focus will often be an outer one with an exact and clear aim. The movement will originate in the extremities and will be experienced as penetrating, cutting gestures, travelling to a clear destination on an undeviating path. Flexible, expanding, shrinking movements or winding paths are a result of indulgent approaches to space.

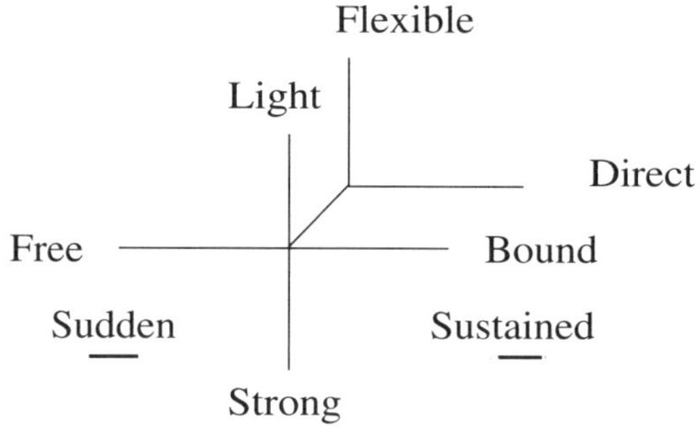

Rudolf Laban's graph of effort assists the verbal and written descriptions of the combinations of motion factors and their importance.

Dynamic qualities are created by the dancer's attitude to the motion factors. These attitudes are as follows:

- a relaxed or forceful attitude to weight
- a flexible or direct attitude to space
- a prolonging or shortening attitude to time
- a liberating or withholding attitude to flow

Every human movement is a combination of several of the above eight elements of movement, but they are more observable in what Laban identified as the "basic actions". He describes them as follows:

A *quick* reaction to an an external stimulus results in four different actions:

Dynamic Actions	*Symbol*
– a direct and strong *thrust*	
– a flexible and strong *slash*	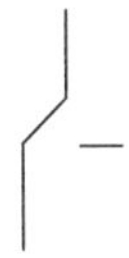
– a direct and light *dab*	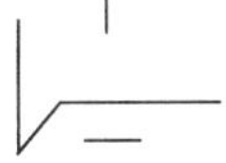
– a flexible and light *flick.*	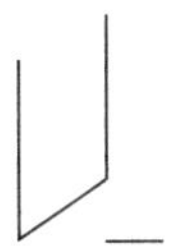

A *hesitation or resistance* can delay the action which becomes sustained and results in four different actions:

Dynamic Actions	*Symbol*
– a direct and strong *press*	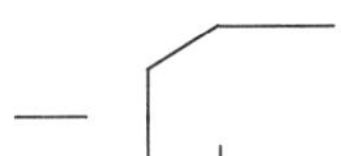
– a flexible and strong *wringing*	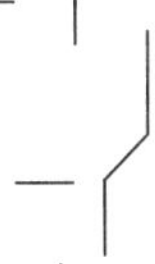
– a direct and light *glide*	
– a flexible and light *float*	

Although Laban's theory of effort is one that relates to everyday human movement, its application to dance movement is obviously possible and enormously illuminating. But what must be remembered, is that as dancers we are *creating* dynamic qualities, whereas as ourselves we *have* them as part of our personalities. A weight, time, flow, space factor is always present in any human movement to some degree. Depending on the degree, it will be a primary or secondary or lesser element of the movement, and will be primarily or hardly perceptible.

Relationships

Preston-Dunlop very clearly lists the basic structures of relationship, as identified by choreology. There are symbols for these relationships in the same way as there are symbols for choreology's identification of actions. Here words will be used to attempt to explain the distinction between one kind of relationship and another: (10)

1. Aware of, focus, addressing
2. Near to, proximity, close but not touching
3. Touching
4. Supporting, taking some weight
5. Surrendering, without touch
6. Surrendering with touch, linking, embracing
7. Carrying, holding, lifting.

There is a development from 1 to 7, and this can be related to human behaviour. In public, focus is used to communicate or address another person. In more social circumstances, closer proximity to another person becomes necessary, and once personal relationships need to function, touch is added to the relationship's communicative structures until surrounding and sharing and taking weight supports intimacy. It is useful for the Latin dancer to use this model to see how the relationship in their five dances functions, how it is created by these structures.

Preston-Dunlop goes on to say that relationships are "always between two, and are initiated or created by both or by one." They can also be held over time or move through space. Obviously, relationships are further created with emphasis on the body, by using the fingertips to touch, or with the emphasis on actions by turning to touch, elevating above or turning away from. When the emphasis is on dynamics, touch can become hitting or grabbing. Direct focus becomes intense, sustained surrounding becomes caring. In this way the dynamic content renders the relationship meaningful. Any change of any movement structures creates a new relationship.

Chapter 7

Basic Characteristics of the Five Latin Dances

This chapter presents the findings of a structural analysis of the five Latin dances. This analysis identifies the primary aspects of the body, the repeated actions, the repeated spatial structures and the necessary and primary dynamic qualities which together characterize each dance and distingish it from the other four. The following information gives details of the very basic characteristics of each dance. An analysis of specific programmes would result in more detailed findings. It is not my intention to confine or restrict the character of the five dances but rather to provide a determined and secure structural basis from which to depart and upon which to build. This analysis is based on the theory presented in the previous Chapter.

Samba

Body: The emphasis is on the flexibility of the torso. The waist, which connects the upper and lower torso (pelvis), allows them to move separately. The movement is generally initiated by the pelvis, which is the centre of gravity, while the upper torso is the centre of levity. The flexibility of the torso is related to the dynamic qualities of the Samba. The arms play only a part in balancing the pulsating torso and should remain secondary and not become over-emphasized.

Action: The recurring actions in the Samba are twisting actions, coupled with contracting and extending (or bending and stretching). In the background, the actions of weight transference and travelling support the choreography of the programme.

Space: The basic figure travels through space, emphasizing not the action of travelling, but the zig-zag floor patterns which serve to give the parading quality to the Samba. Circling in space while travelling or remaining on the spot, is a recurrent spatial structure. (For example, sometimes emphasis is given to the shaping of a "natural roll" and in such cases the movement becomes formal. Whereas, when the emphasis in a "natural roll" is given to dynamics (weight/time), the movement will more likely retain its authentic character.)

Rhythm: The characteristic rhythm of a Samba is created through the alternation of impulse and impact in the phrasing (impulsive and impactive phrasing). On rolls continuous phrasing in the upper body and percussive phrasing of the feet is simultaneously possible.

Dynamics: Giving into gravity is essential and created by "heaviness" in weight. But this has to be coupled with "sudden" movement in time and "flexible" spatial qualities and "free" flow. (Try a "botafogo" starting with an impulse and finishing with an impact on count two of the music. Give the impulse a heavy, sudden, flexible and free quality and the impact a strong, sudden, direct and bound quality.)

Cha-Cha-Cha

Body: The emphasis is on the legs and feet.

Action: The emphasis is on "stepping" which results in the action of gestures of the legs and transferring the weight.

Space: The dance does not travel in its choreographic structure, but remains in one area of the dance floor. The couple moves in opposite and shared directions creating a kind of "dialogue in space", which helps to create the "cheeky" nature of the dance. There is a little more emphasis on shaping the body in space then in the Samba.

Rhythm: The recurrent phrasing of the Cha-Cha-Cha is impactive.

Dynamics: Time is the primary motion factor with sudden qualities predominating. The combination of time/weight qualities is important to create either sudden, strong, direct and bound movements (mostly on steps), contrasting with "sudden, heavy, direct and free" movements (mostly on hip actions).

Rumba

Body:	Physically, the emphasis is given to the hips. The woman emphasizes her hips through movement, tending and focusing an awareness of this effect. The male emphasizes his hips through movement and through awareness of his movement, but focuses on his partner.
Action:	In the Rumba, the walks do not serve to create "travelling", but to serve the weight transference. This weight transference merges with a twisting action and it is the sequential coupling of these two actions that contributes to the essential character of the Rumba.
Space:	Choreographically, the dance does not travel in space but is created in space via the circling, sliding and passing of the couples around, through and in and out of a shared central space. There is more emphasis on shaping and design than in the Samba and Cha-Cha-Cha, although it is the shaping of the dynamics rather than the shaping of the body that creates its essential ever-changing form.
Rhythm:	The Rumba is phrased with alternating movements of impact and impulse with the emphasis on their merging into one another to create continuity in movement. So, although there are accents in the movement phrasing, they do not serve to break the flow but to carry the movement on in a seamless flow of continuous movement.
Dynamics:	This dance gives into gravity with a characteristic movement quality of heaviness, combined essentially with free flow and sustained and flexible qualities (mostly appearing after a walk is taken, while the walk itself is mostly bound, sudden, strong and direct).

Paso Doble

Body:	The emphasis seems to fall on the arms, the elbows, the wrists, the fingers. Also emphasized are the feet, the heels of the feet creating the rhythmic structure and the torso giving the movement its shape and defining the dancer's clear posture. Together the accent on these body parts contributes towards the Spanish character of the Paso Doble.
Action:	While this dance travels through space, its character is created by the recurrent merging of twisting actions into stretching actions.
Space:	This dance is the most shaped of the five dances. The shapes of the body are clearly designed and positional. There is strong spatial tension created between partners. Shapes are created in space through illusionary cape movements and "rondés" (spatial progression), and the shape is further created and consolidated through the use of spatial projection. For example, when the dancers focus directly outwards, their body designs are projected further into space. It is the clearest of all five dances in its floor pattern, because of the relationship between the music and figures, which seems to set the direction of the dance. Three-dimensional movements and positions are a strong focus. Through this emphasis on spatial structures the Paso Doble finds its pride and dignity.

Rhythm: A characteristic rhythm of the Paso Doble is created by the simultaneous percussive phrasing of the feet and the continuous phrasing of the arms and upper body. This contrast in phrasing helps to create the conflict (the drama) within the dance. This conflict (contrast) is a typical characteristic of Spanish Flamenco dance. Meri La: "Here all movements go out from the center (the torso) to curve back into the center; and there is more strength in the 'return' than in the outward movement. If a limb is lifted, there is an almost visible 'pull' to bring it back to the central core." (1)

Dynamics: The main recurrent qualities are in foot placements, direct, strong, sudden and bound; and in whole body actions, direct, strong, sustained and bound. (Try in a Sur Place to increase the energy and strength rather then maintaining time only.)

Jive

Various approaches to the Jive by coaches and dancers today have resulted in two distinct styles; the international style, which is influenced by European cultures (Rock 'n' Roll), and the more authentic style, which has its roots in African-American cultures (Swing).

Body: The gestural kicks and flicks of the legs are emphasized in the international style, while the authentic style adds the torso and hips.

Actions: The characteristic actions of the international style are "gestures", while the authentic style adds the recurring "leaning" and "overbalancing" actions.

Space: Both styles are characterized with partners going to and from a central point and circling it. The central point is created by the hand hold.

Rhythm: The rhythm of the international style is created through recurrent "rebound" phrasing, while the authentic style functions rhythmically in recurrent "swinging" phrases.

Dynamic: The recurrent dynamic qualities which characterize the international Jive are combinations of sudden, direct, light and bound qualitites, while the authentic Jive will combine sudden, flexible, heavy and free qualities.

Table Showing Basic Movement Structures of Each Dance

Dance	Body	Action	Space	Rhythm	Dynamics
Samba	pelvis upper torso	twisting bending stretching	zig-zag circling	impulse/ impact	heavy * sudden flexible free
Cha-cha	legs and feet	"stepping" gesturing transferring weight	shared & opposite direction some design	impact	sudden * strong direct bound
Rumba	hips	weight transfering merging into twisting	sliding passing circling (more de- signing)	impact/ impulse merging continuity	free * heavy sustained flexible
Paso Doble	torso arms feet	twisting merging into stretching	set direction, designed & shaped positions & movements	percussive & con- tinuous	direct * strong sudden bound
Jive Intern.	legs and feet	gesturing	circling and going to and from . . .	rebound	sudden * direct light bound
Jive auth.	legs & feet, - torso & hips	gesturing leaning over- balancing	. . . a central point	swing	sudden * flexible heavy free

* *indicates primary dynamic quality of each dance, see tables below in section* Degrees of Quality.

Characterization

Throughout this book I have reiterated that the participants of all five Latin American dances portray the relationship between a man and a woman, and that this relationship is the subject matter. In the chapters on choreography and creativity I have stressed that the treatment of this subject matter is the precise statement of the dance, which gives it its meaning. The choreography could be called the *movement matter.*

In order to create the character or qualities so essential to each of the five dances, the dancers have to find out what these are, and how they are made visible in performance. This process of characterization is concerned with *movement manner.*

Some Latin American dancers understand characterization to be the narrative of a dance. For instance, general comments are that the Rumba is about a love affair, that the Cha-Cha-Cha is cheeky, that the Samba is a carnival, the Paso-Doble a bull-fight and the Jive is happy. These comments are not totally incorrect in themselves, but, as I have said before, they lead dancers into "acting out" the narrative instead of attending to the movement structures which characterize each dance. In other words, the movement manner.

There is an important sense in which the subject matter, movement matter and movement manner cannot be separated from each other, from the dance itself. For example, the Samba's subject matter, the male/female relationship; its movement matter, that selection of steps recognized as Samba technique arranged and organized by a choreographer; and its movement manner, the dancer's treatment and interpretation and performance of the choreography, collectively create the dance with its particular character.

The following in-depth information provides a theory which may be extremely helpful for dancers who really want to understand the process of characterization in dance.

This chapter generally outlines the main characteristics and interrelationships of different dynamics. Dynamic movement is not something we add to movement, it *is* the movement, in the same way that movement is not added to the person, the person *is* the movement. Laban writes: "The shapes and rhythms which are formed by basic effort actions, movement sensations, incomplete effort, movement drives, give information about a person's relation to his inner and outer world." (1)

In *Mastery of Movement*, Laban explains the following: "The motion factor *space* can be associated with man's faculty of participation with *attention*. The predominant tendency here is to orientate oneself and find a relationship to the matter of interest, either in an immediate, direct way or in a circumspective, flexible one.

The motion factor of *weight* can be associated with man's faculty of participation with *intention*. The desire to do a certain thing may take hold of one, sometimes powerfully and firmly, sometimes gently and slightly.

The motion factor of *time* can be associated with man's faculty of participation with *decision*. Decisions can be made either unexpectedly and suddenly by letting one thing go and replacing it with another one at a given moment, or they may develop gradually by sustaining some of the previous conditions over a period of time.

The motion factor of *flow* can be associated with man's faculty of participation with precision or, perhaps otherwise expressed, *progression*. This is his ability to attune himself to the process of accomplishing, i.e. relating himself to the action. He may control and bind the natural flux of this process or he may give it an unrestricted and free run." (2)

The following table provides a summary of the motion factors, showing how the dancer as a whole person is involved when moving.

A. One Motion Factor

Motion Factor:	Space	Weight	Time	Flow
Inner Participation:	Attention	Intention	Decision	Progression
Concerned with:	Where	What	When	How
Affecting power of:	Thinking	Sensing	Intuition	Feeling

In the study of bodily action, Laban observed that one of the motion factors can be neglected, and only two give the quality or shading to the movement. Laban refers to these as "incomplete effort". They are expressive of a variety of inner attitudes which are interesting for the analysis of Latin dance.

The following illustrates the six incomplete efforts forming three pairs of opposities: (3)

B. Two Motion Factors

Emphasis on Motion Factors	*Giving information about, concerned with*	*Characteristics "inner attitudes"*
Space and Time	Where and When	Awake
Flow and Weight	How and What	Dreamlike
Space and Flow	Where and How	Remote
Weight and Time	What and When	Near
Space and Weight	Where and What	Stable
Time and Flow	When and How	Mobile

If dancers take the trouble to experiment with these combinations, they will discover that the movement will be generally expressive of the attitude or characteristics listed in the right-hand column and can be described as follows:

Awake

That is awareness, certain or uncertain, which may arise suddenly or gradually and may be embracing or concentrated.

Dreamlike

That is unawareness which may be diffused or bold and gloomy or exaulted.

Remote

That is detachment which may include focus on self or universal attention, together with restraint or abandon.

Near

That is presence which may have warm impact or careful consideration, or it may express strong attachment or superficial touch.

Stable

That is steadfastness which may also be resolute and stubborn or sensitively receptive. It may also be solid and powerful or delicately pinpointing.

Mobile

That is adaptability which may be easy or sticky, slowly forthcoming or abruptly changing. (4)

A new set of variations is created by the combination of three motion factors. These are clearly observable when the expression is more pronounced and intense than the inner attitudes of the incomplete actions. When flow is latent, the expression is related to what is identified as "action drive". When weight is not active, qualities emerge representing "vision drive". When time is replaced by flow, a quality of fascination is observable, creating the "spell drive". And finally, when flow replaces space so that spatial qualities are dominant, the particular expression becomes more emotive. In such cases the "passion drive" is created.

C. Three Motion Factors

Motion Factors:	Space, Time, Weight	Flow, Time, Weight	Space, Flow, Weight	Space, Time, Flow
Movement Drives:	Action (Flow dormant)	Passion (Space dormant)	Spell (Time dormant)	Vision (Weight dormant)

This outline of aspects of Laban's theory of effort provides the Latin dancer with knowledge which will allow bodily action (dance movement) to be performed with imaginative awareness, which will enrich the perception and expression of the dynamic content of movement.

The specific application of this theory to the five Latin dances provides the following analysis and information. Each dance, of course, uses all the motion factors, but *which* ones come to the fore and dominate, *which* ones remain in the background and *how* they are combined, serve to create subtle and dynamic characterizations.

Degrees of Quality

In the following tables the symbols " + " and " – " represent increasing or decreasing degrees of the qualities outlined above.

This symbol, for example,
is less strong and
represents a heavy quality.

Samba

	Main	+	With
Motion Factors:	Weight		Time
Inner participation:	Intention		Decision
Concerned with:	What		When
Affecting:	Sensing		Intuiting
		Making	
Two motion factors:		Weight and Time	
Inner attitude:		Near	
		Adding	
Motion Factor:	Space		Flow
Inner participation:	Attention		Progression
Concerned with:	Where		How
Affecting:	Thinking		Feeling
	Foreground	+	**Background**
Three Motion Factors:	Weight/ Time/Space		Weight/ Time/Flow
Drives:	Action		Passion
		Creates Samba	

Characteristics	*Dynamic Quality*	*Symbol*
Main Qualities are:	Heavy/Sudden/ Flexible/Free	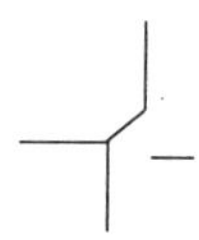
Vigorous Exuberance	= Heavy/Free/Flexible	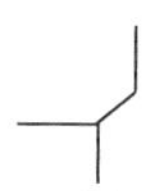
Quick Mental Adoptions	= Sudden/Flexible/Free	
Energy	= Strong/Sudden/Bound	
Striving/Flexibility	= Strong/Flexible/Bound	

Cha-Cha-Cha

	Main	+	**With**
Motion Factor:	Time		Weight
Inner participation:	Decision		Intention
Concerned with:	When		What
Affecting:	Intuiting		Sensing
		Making	
Two motion factors:		Time and Weight	
Inner attitude:		Near	
		Adding	
Motion Factor:	Space		Flow
Inner participation:	Attention		Progression
Concerned with:	Where		How
Affecting:	Thinking		Feeling
	Foreground	+	**Background**
Three Motion Factors:	Time/Weight/ Space		Time/Weight/ Flow
Drives:	Action		Passion
		Creates Cha-Cha-Cha	

Characteristics	*Dynamic Quality*	*Symbol*
Main Qualities are:	Sudden/Direct/ Bound/Strong	
Playful	= Sudden/Flexible/Free	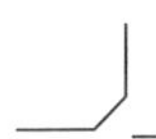
Firm	= Sudden/Strong/Direct	
Alert, Awake	= Direct/Sudden/Free	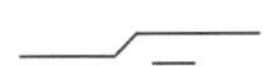
Enterprising	= Strong/Free/Flexible	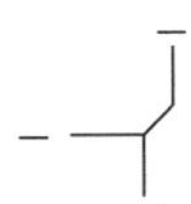

Rumba

	Main	**+**	**With**
Motion Factor:	Flow		Weight
Inner participation:	Progression		Intention
Concerned with:	How		What
Affecting:	Feeling		Sensing
		Making	
Two motion factors:		Flow and Weight	
Inner attitude:		Dreamlike	
		Adding	
Motion Factor:	Time		Space
Inner participation:	Decision		Attention
Concerned with:	When		Where
Affecting:	Intuiting		Thinking
	Foreground	**+**	**Background**
Three Motion Factors:	Flow/Weight/ Time		Flow/Weight/ Space
Drives:	Passion		Spell/Magical
		Creates Rumba	

Characteristics	*Dynamic Quality*	*Symbol*
Main Qualities are:	Free/Heavy/ Sustained/Flexible	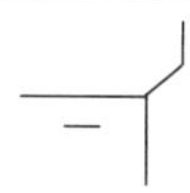
Sensual	= Free/Heavy/Sustained	
Passionate	= Bound/Strong/Flexible	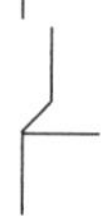
Slow consideration	= Bound/Sustained/Flexible	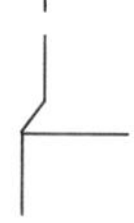
Controlled withholding	= Sustained/Bound/Direct	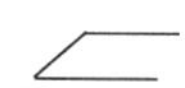

Paso Doble

	Main	+	**With**
Motion Factor:	Space		Weight
Inner participation:	Attention		Intention
Concerned with:	Where		What
Affecting:	Thinking		Sensing
		Making	
Two motion factors:		Space and Weight	
Inner attitude:		Stable	
		Adding	
Motion Factor:	Flow		Time
Inner participation:	Progression		Decision
Concerned with:	How		When
Affecting:	Feeling		Intuiting
	Foreground	+	**Background**
Three Motion Factors:	Space/Weight/ Flow		Space/Weight/ Time
Drives:	Spell/Magical		Action
		Creates Paso Doble	

Characteristics	*Dynamic Quality*	*Symbol*
Main Qualities are:	Direct/Strong/ Bound/Sudden	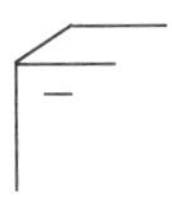
Arrogance, Pride	= Direct/Strong/Bound	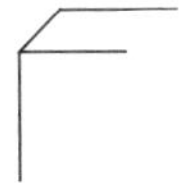
Precision	= Direct/Sustained/Bound	
Restlessness	= Flexible/Sudden/Bound	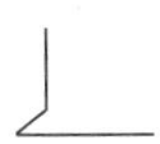
Preparedness	= Strong/Sustained/Bound	

Jive International

	Main	**+**	**With**
Motion Factor:	Time		Space
Inner participation:	Decision		Attention
Concerned with:	When		Where
Affecting:	Intuiting		Thinking
		Making	
Two motion factor:		Time and Space	
Inner attitude:		Awake	
		Adding	
Motion Factor:	Weight		Flow
Inner participation:	Intention		Progression
Concerned with:	What		How
Affecting:	Sensing		Feeling
	Foreground	**+**	**Background**
Three Motion Factors:	Time/Space/ Weight		Time/Space/ Flow
Drives:	Action		Vision
		Creates Jive International	

Characteristics	*Dynamic Quality*	*Symbol*
Main Qualities are:	Sudden/Direct/ Light/Bound	
Lively, Crisp	= Sudden/Light/Direct	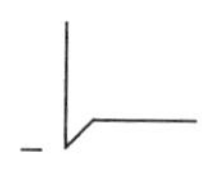
Excited	= Sudden/Free/Flexible	
Spiky, Flicking	= Direct/Sudden/Strong	
Rebounding	= Sudden/Direct/Free	

Jive Authentic

	Main	**+**	**With**
Motion Factor:	Weight		Time
Inner participation:	Intention		Decision
Concerned with:	What		When
Affecting:	Sensing		Intuiting
		Making	
Two motion factors:		Weight and Time	
Inner attitude:		Near	
		Adding	
Motion Factor:	Space		Flow
Inner participation:	Attention		Progression
Concerned with:	Where		How
Affecting:	Thinking		Feeling
	Foreground	**+**	**Background**
Three Motion Factors:	Weight/Time/ Space		Weight/Time/ Flow
Drives:	Action		Vision
		Creates Jive Authentic	

Characteristics	*Dynamic Quality*	*Symbol*
Main Qualities are:	Heavy/Sudden Flexible/Free	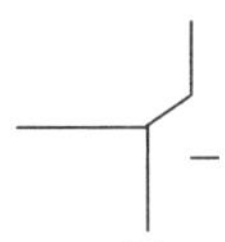
Flexibility	= Heavy/Flexible/Free	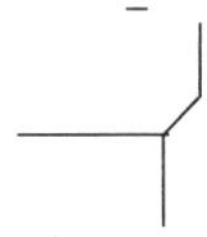
Swinging	= Sudden/Free/Flexible	
Stirring, Slow Twisting	= Sustained/ Flexible/Bound	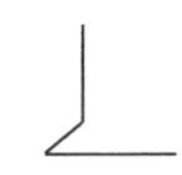
Fluttering, Quick changes	= Sudden/Heavy/Free	

The main purpose of this chapter was to show that characterization is created through the dancer's participation in and commitment to the intrinsic structures of movement and their interrelationship.

The Dramatic Conflict in Dance

The emphasis on how movements are controlled and performed leads to an awareness of the power of expression. For example, attention to the parts of the body and the energy used can help to reinforce change or create dramatic expression. A man *grabs* the *wrist* of his partner and *turns* her to face him. He could *touch* her *hand* and *gently* turn her to face him. This changes the expression. In Latin dance today, at all levels, there is a tendency to "over-dramatize". It should become clear in this section of this book how "devotion to the motion" creates, makes visible and communicates what dances *are* about, what they express, and what their dramatic content might be – and in a way what dancing *is*.

Drama is found in the dance through the dancer's direct understanding and manipulation of movement. But first you have to understand what it is you are manipulating. All the structures of movement outlined in the previous chapter can be directly controlled by the dancer; what part of the body is dominant at a certain moment; what action follows the next or can be combined with another; how the shape is made and perceived; how much or how little energy is required to create just that perfect moment of tenderness or cheekiness and what part you play in the relationship.

Attending to these movement structures gives the dancer more responsibility for creating the dance. It is the dancer's above choices which "make" the dance, not the steps and not the facial expression. This manipulation and choice assists creating the drama in the dancer's performance.

It must be remembered that it is sufficient to create a dramatic context for your performance. In other words your movements need only allude to sexuality or sensuality, you do not have to have sex or act as if you are! This is one of the many instances where the famous artist's saying "Less is more!" applies – and works! To the audience as well as to the judges. By combining structures which do not relate with one another, in other words which are conflicting or in opposition to one another, you will create dramatic moments, for example by combining free flow with direct space, instead of flexible space; by extending arms outwards while contracting centrally and keeping the legs together; by dropping the weight of your pelvis downwards and simultaneously extending arms, head, neck upwards; by taking a flexible path in space but keeping a direct focus on your partner. So many choices will be there for you, offered by your choreography. Drama is not something you add to the dance movement, it's right there staring you in the face. You must learn where to locate it and how to manifest its expression.

Emphasis and Control

Drama can also be created through manipulation of the strands of the dance medium. These strands include those elements of the dance beyond the movement itself, the persons, their costumes and aspects of their appearance, the space, including lighting, decoration and venue itself, and the sound, going beyond musical accompaniment. This idea of conflict between the strands of the medium originates in contemporary theatrical dance. There, opposition creates drama and can be carried to extremes, since the only requirement is that the choreographer's intention is supported.

In most cases in Latin competitive dance, all the strands of the dance medium are emphasized to a point where they all "speak so loudly of the same thing". Collectively, the impact is exhausting, and in a sense we experience a bombardment of the visual, aural and kinetic senses. Whereas, if the costumes for example, were really toned down to something so simple, still conforming to the Latin style but just alluding to it, and if the music was less deafening, this would leave so much room for the dancers to create drama through their movement, without it always being overwhelmed by the other strands.

Of course, the extent to which the dancers themselves can create true opposition within the strands of the medium is limited, because they are not in control of all of them as a theatrical choreographer is. But if the dancers excercised more control over their appearance and their movement, and the institution exercised imaginative and creative control over the space and sound, the dramatic content of both the dances and the competitive occasion could be increased.

Conflict, opposition and attitudes are expressed by the movement of the body and its parts. Rudolf Laban suggests that as a person moves through personal reflections or changing moods he experiences a dialogue between two poles of his individuality. In the same way, conflict and opposition between two or more individuals is in reality a dialogue between two opposite poles. "The duality of the poles becomes visible in movements which display the inner tension." (1) Expression is therefore not added to the movement, but is the movement itself.

Polarities

Connecting these polarities can be a useful notion for the dancer. Tension in the body that pulls upwards and onwards, created by movements or gestures of lightness and ease, will support the grace and romanticism of Standard ballroom dancing, as aspects of that style are made visible. But the same movements, when they connect with strength in the torso and legs, swapping gravity for force, will make conflict, tension, or opposition visible, and will display an aspect of the style of Flamenco dancing, and will no longer be described as romantic, but as dynamic or passionate.

Opposition between two people, between structures of movement, as tension in the body, between two poles of our individuality, between strands of the dance medium all serve to support some degree of conflict, and this conflict is what creates drama in dance. The notion of opposition can thus be used as a tool through which you create dramatic resonance in dance. A misapprehension of this notion can lead to conflict, not of a dramatic kind, but of a disturbing nature which destroys all possibility for creativity.

Strands of the Medium

In a dance performance there is a variety of components which create the performance beyond the movement itself. Although the body's movement is given priority and is the primary medium of dance, the other components play a significant part in their relationship to the whole performance. Valerie Preston-Dunlop identifies the components of the dance performance, or strands of the dance medium, as follows: the movement, the person, the place, the sound. These strands are created by the function of smaller elements. For example, the person strand functions according to the sex and age of the dancer, the costume and all its qualities, hairstyle and props used. The place functions according to the decor, lighting and general atmosphere of the arena or theatre.

Creative Manipulation

A choreographer creating dance for the theatre consciously manipulates the strands of the medium to reinforce the choreographic intention. He is responsible for making all the decisions and choices regarding all the strands of the medium. These chosen strands operate collectively, giving the dance work its identity. For example, it is not only the classical vocabulary and technique that makes "Swan Lake", but the men and women who play the roles of members of Prince Siegfried's court and the women who represent swans. The elaborate and rich textures of the costumes for the members of the court contrast starkly with the pure white feathery tulle of the swans tutus. The stage sets, thrones, staircases, chandeliers, candles and so forth create the court, while the depiction of moonlight on the lake on the backdrop creates the atmosphere for the swans. Two distinct places are created on the same stage space. Tchaikovsky's score carries the narrative and adds audibly to the atmosphere as well as providing a rhythmic relationship with the danced rhythms. If all these strands were changed and only the movement remained, the result would not be "Swan Lake".

The Latin choreographer does not have control of the strands of the medium in the same way. However, the strands are present and operate fully, creating the dances and the competition occasions themselves. It is generally left to the dancers to manipulate the strands of the medium. They decide who they want to dance with. As individuals they create the couple, a tall slender man with a small petite woman, or a short broad-shouldered man with a short well-built woman. Together, they as people create something about the partnership before a movement is made.

There is further manipulation of the person strand via make-up, hairstyles, costume, jewellery. Understanding the essence of your partnership, its strengths and weaknesses, understanding your particular dance programmes, will help to suggest your costume, hairstyle etc. Textures and colours "speak", fabric stretches, hugs tight, swings, falls, and rhinestones *shine*. Think about what you want to present out there on the floor, and choose your costume and manipulate your appearance to enhance your performance and not to distract from it. Make choices that are individual and pertinent to you, do not simply copy others. What suits other people and their dancing might not suit you! Understand the style of Latin dance. You have five different dances within this "style", find a costume that will tolerate all of them, from the Spanish Paso Doble to the North American Jive, but above all choose your costume to suit and enhance you.

It is not necessary to expand on the movement strand here, as it has already been discussed in detail. Suffice it to say that the particular arrangement and organization of the movements which make up your programmes, give your performances their identity in terms of form and content. But in performance movement does not function alone. The interrelationship between those persons dancing, their movement, their costumes, the lighting, the place, the sound, create what we experience as the performance.

Choices and No-Choices

The competitive Latin dance couple are not in a position to manipulate and make choices about the strands we call place and sound. These are made for them. But an experienced dance couple has the opportunity to anticipate how these strands might function on different occasions. For example, will the lighting at the Royal Albert Hall in London create a nightclub atmosphere or will the white lights create a more elegant glamorous environment for your performance? Will the roving spotlights at Blackpool capture your elegance or your dynamism? Will the smaller venue of a more local competition give you an opportunity to exude sensuality in a more intimate setting? In other words, you can have strategies for dealing with these different settings by using them to enhance aspects of your performance. But you cannot do this unless you understand what the strands are and how they function.

In a Latin competition there is more to sound than what the musical accompaniment brings to the performance. Numbers and names are shouted out by excited spectators, there is handclapping, whistling, and from other competitors, stamping, clapping, finger snapping, breathing, hissing, a whole plethora of human sounds and activity which you hear all around you! Again, you have to have a strategy for not only coping with this, but perhaps acknowledging to what degree you will allow the sound to be part of your performance.

An understanding of the nexus of the strands of the medium as the performance itself will give dancers a more informed approach to the choices they can make, and give them access to a unique control over their performances. The choices will allow and encourage individuality and uniqueness, while an understanding of how the strands function will make dancers more aware of the conventions and traditions of the style of Latin dance without being a slave to them.

Strands of the Latin Dance Medium

Persons *Movement* *Place* *Sound*

Persons:	Two dancers male/female, make-up, hairstyles, jewellery, costumes, shoes. The couple is dancing at the same time with other couples, creating the event.
Movement:	Each of the five dances is created by different movement structures which characterize the dance.
Place:	Venue, gymnasium, ballroom etc., size and shape of dance floor, number of competitors, amount of space per competitor, lighting, positioning of judges/audience/dancers. Where does the performance start and finish?
Sound:	Music (live band or recording), shouts, handclapping, whistling, stamping, finger snapping, hissing, breathing, dress, Compère/announcer.

Chapter 8

Beyond Physicality

In my experience as a teacher I have often been confronted with the following problem: the couple I am teaching/coaching readily takes on some ideas, understands the principles behind them, and yet goes out on the dance floor and demonstrates none of it. In an attempt to understand why this happens and to help the dancers, who in all sincerity want to embody new ideas, I have come to understand the important distinction between *habitual* movement behaviour and *automatic* movement.

Does Movement Happen to you, or do you Make it Happen?

As mentioned earlier, our mundane movement behaviour can be described as functional expressive movement, while our dance can be described as aesthetic expressive movement. Functional movement is further described as unconscious spontaneous movement while dance movement is described as conscious deliberate movement. Thus, the nature of our participation in either of these modes of expression is different.

It is within the functional mode that we find habitual behaviour, i.e. doing something constantly, especially as a settled way of behaving. This behaviour is unconscious behaviour and is very hard to change. The deliberate, conscious, intentional dance mode requires the learning and mastering of a specific technique, i.e. skill. Once mastery of a skill is achieved, excecution of skilful movements can become, indeed needs to become automatic, so that the dancers can consciously participate in creating the dance and are not simply doing the dance.

Within dance programmes, when changes are made to programmes which have been known to the dancers and performed by them for years, they will encounter these automatic responses. But with practice, just as the initial programme was learned, new changes can become incorporated and will in turn become automatic, in other words under the dancers' control. But movement behaviour is much harder to change because it is manifested unconsciously. This kind of change, as F.M. Alexander writes, "involves carrying out an activity against the habits of life," not simply changing a physical movement (a turn to the right to a turn to the left), but changing a behavioural response to an outside stimulus.

Is this beyond the realm of the teacher? If the behavioural habits of a dancer are getting in his or her way of controlling the dance, then these things need to be pointed out to the dancer so he or she can at least attempt to address them. Alexander again suggests a reasonable starting point: inhibition, which he defines as the act of refusing to respond, the resistance to an instinct, impulse or feeling. In other words, dancers need to be encouraged to stop in their tracks, to think before doing.

The "thinking" stage of this process can be facilitated in two ways.

Reflection and Visualization

Firstly, "mental imagery" movement occurs in response to ideas. Lulu E. Sweigard writes: "We move because the nerves stimulate the muscles and the muscles move the bones." (1) Therefore, Sweigard argues: "If we change our way of thinking about movement, we will automatically change our neuromuscular response." She called her muscle re-education method *ideokinesis* (ideo for thought, kinesis for motion).

Secondly, creative visualization, which is the use of the imagination to create a clear image of something you wish to manifest, can also be of great benefit to the dancer whose habitual behaviour interferes with the creation of the dance. By focussing on what you want to achieve, it can become an objective reality. This process, if it becomes part of the dancers' practice, will help them to identify their behavioural habits and to recognize when they are extraneous to the dance movement. Thus, the dancers will consciously participate in eliminating habitual behaviour and increase the conscious, intentional, deliberate process of creating their dance.

Unfortunately, the Latin American institution somehow re-inforces both habitual movement behaviour and automatic movement. Firstly, because dancers' repertoires are restricted to their programmes (they do not normally engage in a daily technique or improvisation classes, creative classes in which a variety of movement in the same style can be experienced), the repetition of these programmes over years and years leads to a degree of *automatic* movement that is in danger of losing its freshness. Secondly, the social and emotional influences at work at competitions and on the dance floor are strong external stimuli to which behavioural responses easily fall victim. When nerves take over on the dance floor, all the work in the studio can be overshadowed, even lost. Then *habitual* behaviour, like awkward facial expressions or bland use of dynamics, materialize and come to the fore.

An understanding of the need for skill to be automatic in dance, of the degree of automation which turns dancing simply into doing, and of the distinction between automatic movement and habitual movement behaviour, is essential for dancers and coaches alike if they want to be in control of their dance activities.

You and your Partner

The term implies sharing. A partner is one member of a pair, and the pair implies two vital elements of a shared function, the partnering. In Latin dance, despite the emphasis on the notion of the "male lead", successful partnering is the result of the equal flow of energy between two people, two people dancing *with* each other. If the energy flow is unequal, manipulation results. The manipulator dances *at* the partner, the manipulated dances *for* the partner.

Touch, Sight, Knowledge

One of the most obvious ways of relating to a partner in Latin dance is through touch. The functional aspect of this physical contact is the most obvious, and the one that is constantly referred to. The physical contact can provide momentary support and stability. Besides this functional relationship, touch is meaningful in that, through our tactile sense, we can differentiate between textures and pressure and thus enhance the meaningfulness of the context.

Together with this physical tactile contact, the relationship is created with the use of our visual sense. Don't just look at your partner, *see* him/her! Work on knowing your partner as a person, go beyond the distinction of the particular structure of their face, the colour of hair and eyes, the nose, mouth. Take them in so you are not looking at a strange face. Know your partner and yourself physically, and give this physicality to your relationship, your partnering. Any feelings of self-consciousness will negate both the functional and meaningful aspects of contact.

The sharing of energy, the passing of tension to one another and the reception of this tension from one another, is a highly sensitive function which requires acute understanding if it is to be effectively and subtly mastered. One way of understanding and examining this process is to utilize Laban's theory of contending actions and yielding actions. Basically, contending actions are centrally initiated and send energy outwards. They tend to be bound and strong in dynamic quality and are resisting actions. Yielding actions, on the other hand, are peripherally initiated, release energy inwards, tend to be free and heavy in dynamic quality and are releasing actions. It should be immediately clear how the alternation of these action states within each person perpetuates a flow of energy to and fro, thus supporting an active stream of energy flowing between partners, further creating active and equal partnering.

Before this can be achieved the dancer has to be brought to an awareness of their own physical state. By this, I mean that "neutral" place before perceived movement and contact with another begins. This state is referred to in a variety of ways – a state of readiness, a balanced state of rest, a state of tones, a state of possibility or of potential happening. While this state can be understood intellectually, the physical commitment to it is more challenging. The inner preparation of an outward bodily action requires the ability to relate and adjust to the factors of space, weight and time. As Rudolf Laban says: "The person who has learnt to relate himself to Space, and has mastery of this, has Attention. The person who has mastery of his relation to the Weight factor of effort has Intention, and he has Decision when he is adjusted to Time." (1)

Readiness is all

Thus, the state of potential happening, of readiness, is a state of attention, intention, and decision and, through the flow of movement, becomes a concrete expressive bodily action.

A further aspect of the physical commitment to the state of readiness is related to our three dimensional body structure and its central axis in relation to the force of gravity. The physical challenge lies in finding and experiencing equilibrium. This is an active sensing of balance as potential motion in any direction. If both dancers in a partnership know and experience this state of readiness in the same way, the first contact will be experienced and perceived as a yielding, a flowing into one another, and a unity of motion will be created by their combined action. The ensuing leading and following, contending and yielding, will serve to continue to establish unity. On a directional change, the contending lead of the male dancer will be more readily participated in by the female if such a contact is maintained. From this discussion it is clear that there is a fine line between anticipation and participation. All too often we see couples fighting, each using actions of a sudden, strong and direct quality or "freezing", using sustained, strong and bound actions which serve to separate them and break the unity, or "escaping", using lighter, flexible and free movement by which they appear to disown one another.

Contact does not simply mean two body parts touching. In dance, contact is far more complex because it is motional, not static contact that is being striven for. As cited in the previous paragraphs, the initial fusion is of essential importance, but this fusion needs to continue to function throughout the dance. Because dance is about motion and is active, the contact has to be motional and active. This requires that a connecting stream of energy continues to flow between and within the dancers, actively connecting them to one another. This is one way of ensuring the unity of partnership and of the dance. By taking responsibility for creating the active stream, both dancers will be able to feel and sense their partners as extensions of their functioning selves. Like the blind person's stick, which is an extension of the physical self, feeling, sensing the physical surroundings, you can, through your partner's movements, feel and sense gravity's pull, quality changes, weight transferences, degrees of balance and counterbalance. You should develop this sense to the extent that you feel your partner's foot on the floor, and their transference of weight, as much as you feel your own, by virtue of your shared, felt, activity.

"Unselfishness" and "Leadership" in Dancing

As the blind person feels the ground with a stick, so you should "feel" the ground through your partner. This is absolutely impossible if each partner is "selfishly engaged in their own steps." Using body tension, which supports the individual execution of their separate steps, means that two separately functioning action sequences are being done at the same time, in close proximity, and are perceived as separate. Unity cannot be created until the dancers merge together as one functioning partnership, the ebbing and flowing of energy supporting them individually. For their execution, those individual movements require the very energy that supports the contact. The constant leading and following, ebbing and flowing, arresting and freeing, contending and yielding, is the breath of life for the dance. Until it is understood that the energy needed for the steps to be done, is the same energy that gives the life to partnership, and the same energy that is the dance itself, couples will contrive to dance against each other on the dance floor with a fighting energy that neither serves their partnership nor their "dance".

The above discussion implies that dancing solo is a completely different process from that of a pas de deux, duo or partnership. The emphasis on self can often lead to the destruction of a partnership, or the inability of the partnership to develop at all. But another approach which is detrimental to a partnership is when partners work on one another! It very often happens that men "work" on their female partners. The old notion of leading gives the man the misapprehension that he is the "leader", or like the fisherman, the woman being the fish on the end of his line! It's easy to recognize these partnerships on the dance floor! My warning here is to work on yourselves and you will be working on the relationship, the partnership. Accept one another as individuals with a particular and specific part to play in creating that necessary unity. So often dancers blame one another for tensing up, for not relaxing. As teachers, we so often witness that the one blaming is just as tense because the tension is in the relationship.

With the focus on wanting to win, dancing to win, smiling to win, dressing to win, leading becomes so much a part of that energy, that drive, that goal to win, that it penetrates into the action itself, into the muscles, into the mind and cuts off all sensitivity and watchfulness. One of the problems is that dancers are unaware of this "behaviour" themselves, and as a result do not address it. There is a saying to the following effect: "We are all in prison, but before we can wish to escape from prison, we must first realize that we are there." (2)

In my experience the problem lies not in guiding dancers through the motions of sensitive partnering, but in convincing some dancers that they are victims of this habitual competitive behaviour!

Dominance and Merging

To understand that control of the partnership comes from a merging with one another and not from the dominance of one over the other is quite a difficult notion for some to accept. The following anecdote might persuade some of you. It tells how a famous T'ai Chi master used to feed the birds. He would let them settle, one at a time, on the palm of his hand. When a bird was about to fly away it needed something firm for its feet to press against in order to launch itself. The master was so sensitive and his yielding so refined that he could detect even the tiny muscular effort of the birds legs, and each time it began to push against his palm he yielded just enough to prevent it from flying away. (3) If your partner seems to need time, or you both need to wait or hold time, yield to one another instead of fighting against one another with conflicting energy in order to hold time. What we see in the latter case is not the holding of time but fighting energy.

A physical aspect of controlling partnering involves the use of the elbow, which could be interpreted as the "lever" of the arm, that which gives it play and allows for the arm to be used effectively as the body part which, when pulled on or pushed against causes the whole body/ person to respond. But this only occurs effectively if the one who pulls (usually the man) does not "pull the woman's arm" but pulls her as a whole, and if the one being pulled (usually the woman) responds as a whole. Otherwise arms look as if they are being pulled out of their sockets and the reason for the "pull" is then lost. The position of the elbows in relation to the torso on these push/pull occasions is close to the solar plexus or visualized in relation to the solar plexus, enabling a central yielding of the whole body as a response. In other words, the arm should not stop at the shoulder. If so, there will be a break in the flow of energy and a lack of control and tension will occur.

Developing a sensitive partnership is essential for the Latin American dance couple. When the relationship through physical contact is mastered, further relationships excluding contact will be more readily created and controlled. Shaping one's body in a particular shape can indicate a clear direction of movement for one's partner. The response to this comes from the readiness to perceive it as an invitation to move or even to arrest motion. When the energy between partners is physically shared, it can become mutually visible through dynamic tension in the body.

Internal Strength

Finally, the notion of internal strength can assist the experience of effective partnering. Experts and scientists dealing with sports know that there are many misconceptions about strength and "power". Strength, the target, is of course a state of tension rather than a state of relaxation. But the ability to *achieve* strength is more related to the ability to relax than to the ability to "tense up". In his book *T'ai Chi for Two*, Paul Crompton writes: "Your internal strength will grow the more you relax, the more you become loose.

Internal strength should animate your body (in *T'ai Chi*), not the muscular strength you use to do manual work." (4)

This is a very helpful thought. It implies that strength can be related to yielding and not contending or fighting, i.e. that it is about giving in and not resisting. Therefore it requires the release of tension in the body. Not all energy requires muscular force. The energy that supports effective partnering is related to Crompton's internal strength. It is not about strength (resistance to gravity and your partner's force), but related to giving in to gravity and your partner's energy. In other words, yielding and merging *is* control.

Balance – an Unstable Stability

Another term for balance is equilibrium. Sometimes these words are used to mean the same thing, but essentially they refer to different functions of the same notion. Because of the symmetrical three dimensional structure of the human body we can experience balance through the arrangement of the body and its parts into a particular shape and form which is stable. This is mostly experienced in motion and is perceived in stillness and after a change of support. Then we see balance and feel balanced and stable.

But the human body's natural state is motion. In order for the motion to occur, the stable state needs to lose its line of gravity, tilt the balance into a labile state which will initiate motion. This motion will be "saved" as it passes through stability again and released again as it passes into another labile state. The alternation of stability and lability necessarily creates mobility, and this is known as equilibrium, balance in motion. In other words, walking can be seen as a continuous process of loosing and re-establishing equilibrium, a sequence of "throwing" and "catching" weight.

Labile stances are impossible. Labile movements are movements initiated by weight and gravity. Stable stances can be held. Movements maintaining stability do not lose their line of gravity and are initiated by the control of energy. A form of lability is found in suspension; the next movement is created by a falling in the centre of gravity, causing falling, which is the beginning of the next inevitable movement. A semilabile sensation is experienced in a Rumba Walk as Walter Laird describes it: "To commence a Forward Walk allow the body to move forward with the upper part slightly in advance due to forward poise. Just before point of unbalance is reached, move the left leg forward . . . " (1)

Balance/equilibrium can also refer to the inner harmonic relationship between all the body parts in movement. The symmetry of the body's structure has a potentially harmonic form, and harmony in our culture is related to the concept of balance.

Counterbalance

Balance also introduces the notion of counter-balance. A forward motion is counterbalanced by a motion or pull in a backward direction. An upward pull is counterbalanced by gravity's pull. The opening gestures of the body are counterbalanced by the sequential closing gestures of the body. But the right amount of energy has to be used and controlled in these instances, in order to create and feel equilibrium. In partnering, counterbalance is often used between two bodies, the partner taking over the natural opposition when balancing, like a feeling of hanging from each other or pulling away from each other or leaning towards each other. Through that contact balance is created by your own lability, your partner's lability and the stable form the countertension creates. This is counterbalance.

An awareness of the body's centre of weight, its neutral state or as F.M. Alexander calls it, "a balanced state of rest" and the relationship to gravity will help to develop the sense of balance and equilibrium. An awareness of the space you occupy, i.e., your kinesphere, will allow you to know your space limits for stability and those extensions which move you and your kinesphere into and through general space. Thus, balance/equilibrium is related to spatial perception.

Balance can also refer to an inner psychological balance. Our spiritual, intellectual, emotional, intuitive, physical selves are in a changing relationship with one another, forming a balanced or imbalanced whole. For dancers, the physical self takes priority, but we need to be aware of the whole so that the physical self is in balance with other aspects of our selves. It is often very evident when this is not taken care of.

Rhythm

All life is rhythm. It is the pulse in our blood, our breathing, the underlying element of nature. It is seen in the movements of the seasons, the passing of day and night, in the whole vast rhythm of a transient world. It is perhaps for this reason that we seem to have an unconscious desire to organize sounds. For example, when we hear a tap running and hear every drop as a beat, we tend to measure them and hear an accent that is in fact not there. In music, there are of course accents, bars and "beats". But we should not simply identify rhythm with beats and bars.

All too often, rhythm is understood as timing: as something to do with time only. While time is an essential structure of movement, it is not the only structure. Rhythm to a dancer has an extra dimension. Information is necessary, e.g. with the statement "step one on count one": the rhythm of the steps in relation to the music can be metrically counted out and given. But until the days of counting are over, "dance" cannot happen. Because music is often used as the basis for the rhythmic structure of the dance and the stimulus for the dancer, it is all too easy to fall into the trap of mimicking the metric structure of the music with mechanical movements of the body (i.e. steps).

Body rhythms relate to the structure of our body and to the structural components of our movement. These operate together in a complex relationship and understanding this relationship allows us to identify the structures of movement rhythm as distinct from heard rhythm, and might deepen our understanding of the notion of our musicality.

Alma Hawkins writes the following about rhythm: "As an organizer, rhythm might be thought of as a potent force that binds together the various elements of dance into a unified and harmonious structure." (1)

The "structural components of movement" or the "various elements of dance" Hawkins refers to are identified by choreology as body, actions, space, dynamics and relationships. When the dancer consciously changes one or more of these structures, this change affects the whole. For example, changing an arm-movement to a movement of the hand only, changing the action of travelling to the action of stillness or turning, changing the quality of the movement from lightness to heaviness, changing a movement *through* space to one *in* space, or changing movement toward your partner to one away from your partner; all these changes following one another in a particular organization effectively result in structuring the rhythm of the movement. One could say that rhythm is the way the structures of movement interrelate in a changing process.

So, to create different rhythms we can concentrate on one or two structures of movement which will bring those elements to the fore, i.e. they are clearly felt by the dancer and clearly perceived by the spectator. The other elements are there but not primarily felt and perceived.

Spatial and/or Dynamic Priorities

Two examples from the Latin repertoire clearly demonstrate this point. In the Paso Doble the spatial structures of the movement are essential for shaping the dance to help create the necessary pride and arrogance. By concentrating on these elements of the movement, the other structures fall into a new relationship with each other, refining their organization and creating a rhythm specific to that organization.

The Samba on the other hand requires an exuberant atmosphere, liveliness and gaiety. Concentration on the dynamic elements bases the movements on a rhythm that is essentially dynamic, while the action elements and body elements follow, and the spatial elements remain secondary in terms of creating this specific and essential rhythm. This discussion indicates that rhythm is a highly complex notion, when referring to human movement, and that the essential focus is change.

Timing and Speed

In Latin there is a tendency to think of rhythm as two-three-four-and-one or slow-slow-quick-quick or two-and-three-and-four-and-one etc. This stepping on musical counts is named "timing" and refers only to the speed of the steps. Even if we understand rhythm only as timing, the question remains, what is it that changes? For example, on slow-slow-quick-quick it is not just a matter of waiting longer on the slow step in relation to the quick step, but of controlling the speed and duration of the slow step. Movements are not simply fast or slow.

The speed of our movement is controlled by the amount of energy we use, and when we change that we create changes in rhythm. Because of the way our movements flow from one to another, the way they are put together and organized, the end of one movement becomes the beginning of the next, and what can be learned essentially as a single step on a single count of music becomes a movement which itself changes speed during its execution either accelerating or decelerating, requiring energy to be arrested or released. Some movements and steps take longer to happen than others, they have different durations as well as speeds. Changing the speed, or duration of a movement or set of movements, or changing structures of movement results in "accents" being felt and perceived. These accents serve to punctuate the flow of movements, organizing the energy so that rhythm is experienced, felt and made visible.

Choreological Terms

Choreology has identified these changes. Taking into account the change in speed, the duration and creation of accent. The following terminology might prove helpful for an understanding of rhythm in movement. (3)

Term / Symbol	***Description***
Impulse: 	Impulse describes a movement that has an accent at its beginning, because that is where its greatest speed is seen and felt, after which the greatest change is seen or felt. The movement decelerates over time.
Impact: 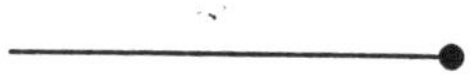	Impact is the opposite of impulse. Accent and greatest speed are at the end of the movement, while the movement begins at a speed that continues to accelerate throughout its duration.

Swing:

The accent of a swing is centrally placed, in that the beginning and end of a swinging movement are suspended, while the greatest speed, the greatest change, in this case the dropping of weight, occurs in the middle of the movement.

Constant:

Many movements do not have accents or changes of any kind and are controlled throughout their duration.

Vibration:

The accent is on every movement with an irregular speed, controlled through a constant interplay between tension and release. Trembling actions are examples of vibration.

Percussive:

The accent is on every movement which tends to create a clear rhythmic structure.

Rebound:

A rebound is an impact followed by an impulse but merged into one movement with one accent.

Suspension:

Suspension is a movement that decelerates until the next movement must inevitably result from it.

Body – Rhythm – Phrase

These examples describe the rhythm of single movements, but in dance we do not do single movements. We relate one movement to the next. This progressive relationship of one movement to the next is called phrasing. In Latin, phrasing is again related to the structure of the music, e.g. an eight bar phrase. But what about the structure of movement? In movement, phrasing is the relationship of changes in an organic unity. The organic unity is the structure of the arrangement of those changes.

The linguistic model supports this understanding of phrasing. A specific arrangement of letters creates words, the arrangement of words creates sentences, sentences create prose. For example the "Hockeystick" in Rumba on its own is like a word without a sentence. It is what follows and precedes which gives a word as well as the hockeystick, rhythm and phrasing. It is rhythm and phrasing that contribute to meaning.

A body rhythm phrase creates the smallest compositional unit of dance in which actions are combined rhythmically in a set form, resulting in a closed choreographic pattern. As a rule, they are bound in a dynamic arch: for example, the relationship of actions and dynamic:

Actions:

Dynamic:

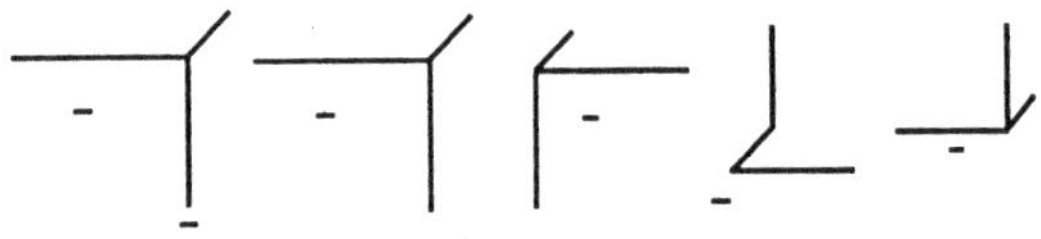

When the movement phrase is not identical to the musical phrase it does not mean that they are unrelated. Being musical does not mean that your movement rhythm is the same as the audible music rhythm. A dancer's awareness of his responsibility to create, that is to phrase his dance movement, coupled with his ability to relate that to the music rhythm is what musicality in dance entails. The interrelationship between the two rhythms is musicality, whether their relationship be identical or complementary.

The Couple as Meeting Place

Beyond their relationship to the music, Latin dancers have to understand the many levels on which their partnership (their rhythm relationship to their partner) is created. It is neither necessary nor even common for a male dancer to share the same movement phrasing as his female partner. But unless each one is clear about their own rhythm there can be no "meeting place", no relationship, no rhythm to their dance and little hope of relationship with the music.

A. The *music phrasing* can be:

B. The *male body rhythm* phrasing can be:

C. The *female body rhythm* phrasing can be:

The interrelationship of A, B and C creates the dance phrase.

But dancers and teachers can enhance this sensitivity to movement rhythm by not always counting the musical counts, but by providing a verbal accompaniment of dynamic sounds which generate the changing qualities within a phrase or phrases of movement. In this way physical sensing of rhythm can be encouraged.

Audiences as well as judges perceive rhythm kinesthetically, i.e. consciously or unconsciously within the aesthetics of movement. They feel the underlying regular pulse, the repetitions, the accents and progression from one phrase to the next, creating a harmonious relationship. The dancers can only include the audience participation in their rhythms if they are aware of creating them.

When the audience senses that the rhythm is only a matter of changing without movement, phrasing the perception of it becomes chaotic, changing for the sake of changing. Their unconsious desire to organize sounds and to seek form in the rhythm then remains unfulfilled.

The "Centred" Human Being

Generally, when one speaks about centring or being centred in dance, it is the physical centring, balancing, equilibrium of the body's weight in relation to the forces of gravity that is referred to. The three dimensional structure of the body is in itself a balanced structure and has its own central point which is located in the middle of the back and a few centimetres below the navel. This is the centre of contraction and release and is the central point of the body's verticality, the central line of gravity. The centre of gravity in the human body is located in the region of the pelvis. This is the centre of weight. When the body is properly aligned and balanced in its verticality, the vertical line of gravity (as seen from the side) passes just behind the ear, through the shoulder, the middle of the hip, and continues in front of the ankle and through the foot.

The centre of *levity* refers specifically to the region of the sternum of the upper trunk. This is the centre of lightness, which by virtue of its location in the sternum is vertically related to the centre of weight in the pelvis. Both these centres activate motion and are the centres from which outward movement of the limbs is initiated and to which their movements return.

The Moving Centre

Further physical centres can be located in body parts. For example, when the arms are held horizontally outwards to the side of the body and the energy is released in the arm, gravity will initally seem to take the elbow downwards. It could be said that in such movements the centre is the elbow. The centre of body parts in gestural movement, it seems, is often experienced in the joints.

The centre in partnering is a moving one. It is often located in the handhold, when that physical contact of meeting occurs. The partnering centre can be located at that point where shoulder meets shoulder, ankle meets ankle, head meets chest. This meeting point is the central point where partners receive information. They sense how much to yield, when to move in response, how to approach, how and when to react. The centre of a dancing partnership is always changing, always moving.

The term centring and centred also alludes to the centring of the dancer as a whole being, and not just dancer as physical body weight and structure. Dancers are physical, emotional, intellectual, intuitive and spiritual beings, and we strive for a balance with respect to our complex make-up. These aspects of ourselves are less tangible than the physical, but are no less important. There are many theories and practices which support the holistic approach to the human being. In Eastern philosophy Chakra is the name given to an energy centre in the body. Chakra is a sanskrit word for "wheel" and these centres are understood to be the centre of a wheel of functioning energy.

Chakras

The major chakras, usually considered to be seven in number, lie along the spine, from its base to the top of the head.

1. The *Root Chakra* is centred on the coccyx, at the base of the spine and is related to our survival instinct.
2. The *Sacral Chakra* is rooted in the sacrum and is related to our emotion, pleasure and nourishment.
3. The *Solar Plexus Chakra*, located between the navel and the bottom of the ribcage, is the largest and most powerful of the chakras. Isadora Duncan referred to this centre as the soul. This chakra is related to power, achievement and success.
4. The *Heart Chakra* is the central chakra of the body, balancing the energies of the lower chakras through acceptance. As the energy of the Heart Chakra develops, it allows more energy to flow through the upper chakras. This chakra is related to love and acceptance.
5. The *Throat Chakra* deals with communication and our creativity. In other words the way we express ourselves in the world.
6. The *Eye Chakra* deals with the way we see and understand the world. Our ability to visualize and analyze comes from this chakra.

7. The *Crown Chakra* is the spiritual centre of the body and the centre through which the cosmic energy of the universe most powerfully enters the body. This centre relates to our holism, autonomy and, in religious terms, divinity.

This system appeals to me because it sees the chakras in relation to different kinds of activity. On one level, the energies of the chakras form the physiological and psychological make-up of a person (each chakra has a personal psycho-physical quality), and on another level each chakra can operate on a mental level. This deals with the way we receive energy coming from other people and the outside world, and how we psychically project our own energy. This energy belongs to a phenomenon which seems to be beyond the physical. So, while Argyle's signals help us to communicate on the non-verbal but physical level, awareness of the chakras assists in the understanding of that formless feeling energy through which we communicate, and which in some way can be felt and even "seen".

Besides giving access to the understanding of this virtual energy, the locations of the chakras provide for distinction of the different levels within the torso, which might otherwise not be recognized. For example, the lower torso (the pelvis), which is the centre of gravity, contains the root and sacral chakras. These chakras are related to our survival instinct and to the nourishment of emotions and pleasure respectively. These chakras suggest our physical needs and a correlation could be drawn here with C.G. Jung's physical aspect of self as well as Laban's weight factor.

The next two chakras, the Solar Plexus and Heart Chakras are located in the upper torso (chest), the centre of levity. These chakras are related to our power of achievement and success, to love, acceptance and holism respectively. It is interesting to draw the correlation here with Jung's emotional aspect of self and Laban's flow factor.

It is not by accident that Delsarte divided the torso into three parts; the lower "doing", the middle "feeling" and the upper (head) "thinking" part of the self. The last three chakras are located in the throat and head. Their relation with our expression, our vision and our spirituality correlates neatly with Jung's intellectual aspect of self, Laban's Space factor and Delsarte's thinking.

Torso	**Chakra location**	**Chakra energy**	**Jung**	**Laban**	**Delsarte**
Lower	root		survival		
torso	coccyx	instinct			
(pelvis)			physical	weight	doing
Centre	sacral	emotional			
of	sacrum	pleasure			
gravity		nourishment			
Upper	solar	power			
torso	plexus	achievement			
(chest)		success			
			emotio-	flow	feeling
Centre		love	nal		
of	heart	acceptance			
levity		holism			
Neck	throat	creative			
		communi-			
		cation			
and		expression			
			intellec-	space	thinking
	eye	vision	tual		
Head	crown	spirituality			

Awareness as a Tool

In my experience as a teacher, I have found that my increasing awareness of this notion of centring helps me to be more sensitive and subtle in my approach to dancers as whole beings. Sometimes I have found it appropriate to use this terminology to ellicit a required response from a dancer. It is more subtle, less tangible, but because it requires the dancer to reach into the depths and secrets of their own being, the movement is charged with an energy that comes directly from them and is more likely to be centrally and clearly felt and perceived by both partner and spectators.

When leading in partnering, with or without touching, it is possible to focus on a specific chakra centre. Feel the difference on opening a Rumba on count two with an awareness of the lower chakras of the torso and on closing on count four with an awareness of the upper chakras of the torso. A literal translation of this suggestion might easily lead to its crass treatment and application. I am not suggesting that focussing on energy from chakra number one will result in effect number ten! What I am aware of is that the stream of energy, referred to so often in this book as free or bound flow, is only a part of the energy system which is the human being.

My understanding of this has given me insight into how we function as individual human beings. The acknowledgement of chakra centres offers a method of exploring the multi-dimensional aspects of being human. The treatment of dancers as human beings, with private lives which cannot be separated from their "dancing lives", continues to open up the possibilities of change and growth and development in their dance.

I am aware that the philosophy of chakras incorporates a practice, a way of life, and that activating these energy centres is a private, meditative, ongoing life experience. To me the value of discovering this philosophy lies in its clear physical location of centres in the torso. Awareness of the chakras and their psycho-physical qualities leads to a fuller sensing of changing energy and to the perception of that change. For dance, this can be helpful in dealing in a more direct way with these less tangible but ever present aspects of the dance.

APPENDIX

A. Historical Development of Views on Expression

The problem of expression in dance is not a new one. Throughout the 400 year evolution of classic theatrical dancing, practioners and theorists have offered their views on expression. This century the parallel development of modern dance has further questioned expression in dance. The development of both genres is characterized by swings towards the notion that technique is the vehicle of expression, therefore an absolute necessity, and towards the idea that no technique or skill is necessary for expression to function in dance.

Different opinions and practices have influenced the development of dance itself. The following examples give a brief indication of these ideas and serve as a reminder that, although in Latin we might embark on a process of discovering expression for ourselves within our style and genre, we do not have to "reinvent the wheel" as it were. What is essential is that our approach is informed by the past.

A choreological approach to dance presumes the adoption of some of Rudolf Laban's theories on human movement and is the primary approach used in this book. To complete the picture and to contextualize Laban (1879 – 1958) as a theorist, the following discussion briefly introduces theorists and dance practitioners from the later 19th and 20th centuries who have influenced today's attitude toward dance.

Francois Delsarte, a French philosopher (1811 – 1871) developed and taught what he termed "the laws of expression" on the trinitarian basis that human beings comprise intellectual, emotional and physical divisions. His pseudo-scientific theories articulated principles, whereby humans give form to feeling through the body, and further allowed for the classification of each bodily gesture in terms of an emotional significance. Delsarte's teachings served as a philosophical and physical basis for dance students especially in America, where his influence was one of the origins of "Modern Dance".

Musicologist Curt Sachs also developed a theory of expression in dance, in which he attempted to formulate universal patterns. But his theory today becomes problematic as he compared "ritualistic movements of nonhumans with the dance of humans." (1)

Susanne K. Langer, a prominent philosopher of dance in this

century, provides for the understanding of the transformation of ideas or the structure of feeling into symbolic forms. She objects to the notion that gesture springs from actual feeling. She puts forward the idea that "it is imagined feeling that governs the dance not real emotional conditions," and that "it is actual movement but virtual self-expression." (2)

As far back as the 18th century Jean-Georges Noverre believed that the "language of dance was universally understood." Writing in 1760, that "a well composed ballet is a living picture of the passions, manners and customs and ceremonies of all nations of the globe." Later in the 1890's the continuing argument between technique and expression provoked Lois Fuller's remarks, "the moment you attempt to give dancing a trained element, naturalness disappears. Nature is truth, art is artificial." Following her, Isadora Duncan pre-occupied with the solar plexus as the central spring of all movement, expressed her deep personal emotions in her dances, trusting her body to tell her what she needed to know as a dancer.

Michel Fokine (trained at the St. Petersburg School of the Imperial Russian Ballet) was struck by Isadora's dancing. It revealed to him the beauty and grace of the natural human body uncluttered by technique. He believed that the ballet had denounced expression, had become mechanical due to an overreliance on technique. He tried to remedy the situation by advocating the study of one's own body, providing principles which suggested an emotional expressiveness. This attitude was previously unheard of in the Russian Ballet.

Vaslav Nijinsky (1888 – 1950) continued this line of thought especially in his ballets *L'apres Midi d'un Faun*, *Le Sacre du Printemps*, *Jeux*, where he attempted to make audiences "feel" his work saying "I think little and therefore understand everything I feel. I am feeling through the flesh and not the intellect."

Ruth St. Denis, American Modern Dance pioneer of the early 1900's, viewed the body as the physical manifestation of the spiritual condition. Both St. Denis and Ted Shawn were influenced by Delsartes' system. Mary Wigman (1886 – 1973) assumed that the human body could mirror spiritual states of being and that dance was a language understood by all human beings. Martha Graham (1894 – 1991), pioneer of American historic Modern Dance, developed a technique which allowed for the "stylized movements to be expressive of passionate, emotional states and violent crisis of spirit." Hers was a direct reaction against ballet's aesthetic, which, in her opinion, could not express the feelings and the awareness of 20th century human kind.

Alwin Nicholais (born 1912) attempted in his choreographic works to wipe out any vestiges of personal emotion, while Georges Balanchine of the NYCB attracted labels from critics such as "abstract and formal". He deliberately de-emphasized the tendency to express emotion and evoke emotion in the audience by emphasizing the manipulation of movement itself. Choreographers of the 60's and 70's emphasized what they called "naturalness", which to them meant draining movement of emotional overlay. This movement went consciously against earlier traditions by seeking to integrate physical experience with the doing of the dance. Merce Cunningham relieved dance movement of the burden of meaning, preferring to concentrate on movement for its own sake.

Later, the Judson Dance Theatre group in the 60's freed dancing from technique and the overt virtuosity of Cunningham's and Balanchines's performances, believing that the trained body burdened with a particular style hid the real beauty of naturalness and spontaneity of movement. Thus, ordinary people performed pedestrian movements on stage in what was called "dance." Yvonne Rainer, the most prolific of the Judson Dance Theatre choreographers formulated a "strategy of denial" whereby she attempted to "demystify" dance: "No to spectacle, no to virtuosity, no to transformations and magic and make believe, no to the glamour and transcendency of the star image, no to the heroic, no to trash imagery, no to involvement of performer or spectator, no to style, no to camp, no to seduction of spectator by the wiles of the performer, no to eccentricity, no to moving or being moved." (3)

Further on into the 70's, choreographers Paul Taylor, Eric Hawkins, Alwin Ailey sought to reset the balance, again seeking an emotional response from their audiences. They did this by drawing on folk and ritual traditions as models to help restore the lack of vitality in the dance theatre.

"If other people want to analyze what I do, that's fine with me . . . but I won't. It has too much to do with instinct, feelings, your personal experience in dance and outside it. It is life. It is much too mysterious to begin to understand." (4)

Dance performance has continued to change and develop at a seemingly increased rate during the 80's and early 90's, and from where we stand now, reflection on these movements is difficult as we are part of them. However, the 80's could be characterized by concerns about cultural differences, social consciousness and political attitudes which have become evident in the theatre. The 90's seem to be driving these attitudes even deeper. Stephen Petronio's "uncontrolled body is a demand for the rights to non-conformism, to individuality," and Lloyd Newson's works energetically bravely and dangerously "deviate" and strike at the heart of the political and the personal. (5)

In this brief summary I hope to have shown how attitudes towards the body and its expression dominate the development of dance performance, and that theoretical issues are not a recent phenomenon in this field. I am not suggesting that, unless we understand intellectually or react analytically to dance performance, we cannot appreciate it. I am suggesting that to reflect on and contemplate these ideas brings special insights and knowledge to the individual, whereby teachers, coaches, dancers and judges can reach their goals more effectively.

B. Concepts of Creativity

One of the most successful, reliable and exciting ways to encourage the acquisition of open skills is the development of creativity. But before creativity can be nurtured, and open skills discovered and developed, a safe trusting atmosphere has to be created.

Creativity is probably present to a greater or lesser degree in all human beings. It is an elusive phenomenon, occurring not only in art, but in all activities that reach out, seek and search for new horizons, relationships and objects. Lois Ellfelt presents the following as characteristic responses to the question of what is meant by "creativity":

1. The generation or development of an objective product
2. A single act of personal discovery
3. Anything fresh or new
4. Rearrangement of the old
5. Development or variation
6. Solution to any problem
7. Identification of something worth bothering with
8. Process of search resulting in a product
9. A part of living
10. Pointing out new relationships. (1)

It is probably impossible to find any universally acceptable criteria for all concepts of creativity, and whether it is related to a process or product is immaterial.

Here are some views on creativity. Amy Lowell compared the start of creativity to "the idea dropped into the subconscious, like a letter into the mailbox." Rollo May wrote that creativity was an "encounter of the intensively conscious human being with his world." Jerome Bruner called it "effective surprise." Eric Fromm said it was the "ability to see and respond." Arthur Koestler called it "emotionally charged participation and discovery." (2)

From all the above views and responses, one could generally consider creativity to be the drawing of something into existence, entailing an outpouring controlled by a critical mind. The origin of the creative process, as psychologist Guilford suggests, is the response of the imagination to sensory perceptions, and the key to the creative personality is the ability to be sensitive to one's surroundings.

Making dance is a creative process which is product orientated. L. A. Reid writes that creativity fuses the cognitive with the affective. The cognitive is traditionally concerned with thinking matters, and the affective is concerned with feeling matters. Creative activity is related to an "imagined conception" (3) because the artist does not foresee the final result of the activity.

This is a function of openness and drive, a product of rich experience, self-confidence, sensitivity, and a willingness to be, as well as to become.

The crux of the creative process lies in the freedom from superimposed ideas and convention. Conformity itself restricts, orders and controls, while creativity fosters freedom, experimentation, expression and facility, along with vitality and energy of the imagination. (4)

Central to the creative process is the ability to break with convention, break and bend the rules, dismiss tradition and to be brave enough to follow what the imagination dictates.

Notes and Bibliography

Notes

Chapter 1

Competitive Latin American Dance

1. *Tanzspiegel*, Nr. 7, July 1989.
2. *Dance News*, ed. 1164, Oct. 18, 1990.
3. *Dance Beat*, July 1990.
4. Rijn, D., *Encyclopedie van de Sport*, Helmond, Holland 1960, page 9.
5. Reid, Louis Arnaud, Article on *Sport, The Aesthetic and Art*, 1976.

6/7. Ibid. page 6.

8. Ibid. page 8.
9. Ibid. page 9.
10. Ibid. page 12.
11. Ibid. page 124.
12. Ibid. page 11.
13. Ibid. page 16.

14/15. Ibid. page 20.

Competition

1. Brown, J. M, *The Vision of Modern Dance*
   Publ.: Princeton Book Company, Princeton 1979, Hanya Holm Speaks, page 73

The Question of Authenticity

1. Martin, John, *The Dance in Theory*
   Publ.: Dance Horizons Princeton 1965, page 76.
2. La Meri, *Total Education in Ethnic Dance*
   Publ.: Marcel Dekker, New York 1977, page 17.

Chapter 2

Institutional Structures

1. Fraleigh, S. H., *Dance and the Lived Body*
   Publ.: Pittsburgh Press, Pennsylvania 1987, page 58.

Technique

1. Sorrel, W., *Hanya Holm*
   Wesleyan University Press, USA 1969, page 155.

2. Ellfeldt, Lois, *Dance from Magic to Art*
   Publ.: Wm. C. Brown, USA 1976, page 203.

Judging

1. Adshead, Janet, *Dance Analysis: Theory and Practice*
   Publ.: Dance Books, London 1988, page 90.

2. Ibid. page 91.

3. Ibid. page 98.

4. Ibid. page 99.

5. Ibid. page 99.

Chapter 3

Expression – Feeling – Emotion

1. Langer Susanne K., *Feeling and Form*
   Publ.: Charles Scribner's Sons, New York 1953, page 67.

2. Ibid. page 26

3. Hanna, J. C., *The Performer-Audience Connection*
   Publ.: University of Texas Press, Austin 1983, page 18.

4. Langer, Susanne K., *Feeling and Form*
   Publ.: Charles Scribners's Sons, New York 1953, page 67.

5. Hanna J. C., *The Performer-Audience Connection*
   Publ.: University of Texas Press, Austin 1983, page 27.

6. Ibid. page 36.

7. Ibid. page 37.

8. Doubler, N. H., *Dance a Creative Art Experience*
The University of Wisconsin Press, London 1957, page 23.

Abstraction

1. Shawn, Ben, *The Shape of Content*
Harvard University Press, USA 1957, page 62.

2. Martin, John, *The Modern Dance*
Publ.: Dance Horizons, New York 1965, page 42.

3. Bellido, R.T., *Kandinsky*
Publ.: Bracken Books, London 1987, page 44.
(The painter Wassily Kandinsky neatly reinforces the necessity of keeping the unnecessary out of art: "I could never employ forms by proceeding from logical processes, only those born within me by an inner necessity. The form of a horse becomes more magical the further I depart from an actual horse.")

4. Hawkins, A. M., *Creating through Dance*
Publ.: Dance Horizons Books, New Jersey 1969, page 96.

Form and Content

1. Langer, Susanne K., *Feeling and Form*
Publ.: Charles Scribners's Sons, New York 1953, page 67.

2. Martin, John, *Introduction to the Dance*
Publ.: W. W. Norton & Company Inc., New York 1939, page 59.

3. Shawn, Ben, *The Shape of Content*
Publ.: Harvard University Press 1957, page 70.
("For Form is not just the intention, it is the embodiment of content. Form is based, first upon a supposition, a theme. Form is, second, a marshalling of materials, the inert matter in which the theme is to be cast. Form is, third, a setting of boundaries, of limits, the whole extent of an idea, but no more, an outer shape of idea. Form is next, the relating of inner shapes to the outer limits of the theme. It is the abolishing of excessive materials, whatever material is extraneous to inner harmony, to the order of shapes now established. Form is thus a discipline, an ordering, according to the needs of content.")

Chapter 4

Dance Education

1. Huang, Al, *The Essence of TaI JI*
   Publ.: Celestial Arts, California 1987, page 14.
2. Peters, R. S., *What is an Educational Process?* In R. S. Peters, *Concept of Education*
   Publ.: Routledge and Kegan Paul, London 1967, page 6.
3. Ibid. page 18.
4. Brinson, Peter, *The changing Nature of Dance studies*
   Dance Studies, ed. Roderyk Lange, Vol. 3, 1978/9, page 71.
5. Hawkins A.M, *Creating through Dance*
   Publ.: Dance Horizons Books, New Jersey 1969, page 95
6. Huang, Al, *The Essence of TaI JI*
   Publ.: Celestial Arts, California 1987, page 20.
7. Ibid. page 52.
8. Ibid. page 63.
9. Schmidt, R.A, *Motor Control and Learning*
   Human Kinetics Publishers, Illinois 1988, page 460.
10. Peters, R. S, "What is an Educational Process?" in *Concept of Education*
    R.S. Peters, (Routledge and Kegan Paul, London 1967) page 20.
11. Ibid. Page 21.
12. Hawkins, A.M, *Creating through Dance*
    Publ.: Dance Horizons Books, New Jersey 1969, page 19.
13. Ibid. page 18.
14. Ibid. page 117.
15. Ibid. page 118.
16. Ibid. page 120.

Creativity

1. Hawkins, A. M., *Creating through Dance*
   Publ.: Dance Horizons Books, New Jersey 1969, page 7.

2. Rogers, Carl, "Towards a theory of creativity" in *Creativity and its Cultivation*
   ed. Anderson, page 78-80.

3. Hawkins, A. M., *Creating through Dance*
   Publ.: Dance Horizons Books, New Jersey 1969, page 15 f.

Choreography

1. 1974 *Yearbook of the International Folk Music Council,* Chapter on Foundations for the analysis of the structure and form of Folk Dance: a syllabus.

Chapter 5

Non-Verbal Communication

1. "Popular Arts," *The New Encyclopedia Britannica*

2. Hanna, J. C., *The Performer-Audience Connection*
   Publ.: University of Texas Press, Austin 1983, page 27

3. Argyle, Michael, *Bodily Communication*
   Publ.: Methuen & Co. Ltd, New York 1975, 2nd ed., preface

4. Ibid. page 1.

5. Ibid. page 88.

6. Ibid. page 97.

7. Ibid. page 100.

8. Ibid. page 102.

The Treatment of "Male" and "Female" in Latin American Dancing

1. *Dance Beat*, Nov. 1992, page 7.
2. Hanna, Judith Lynne, *Dance, Sex and Gender*
   University of Chicago Press, 1988, page 157.
3. Model based on one presented by Judith Lynne Hanna, *Dance, Sex and Gender*
   University of Chicago Press, 1988, page 160-161.

The Comparative Nature of Movement

1. Lamb, Warren and Watson, Elizabeth, *Body Code. The Meaning of Movement*
   Publ.: Princeton Book Company, Princeton 1979, page 47
2. Ibid. page 42.
3. Ibid. page 86.
4. Ibid. page 90.

Chapter 6

The Intrinsic Structures of Movement

1. Preston-Dunlop, Veronica, *Dance is a Language, isn't it?*
   Publ.: Laban Center for Movement and Dance, London, 3rd ed. 1987, Chapter on Body.
2. Ibid. Chapter on Body.
3. Ibid. Chapter on Body.
4. Ibid. Chapter on Action.
5. Ibid. Chapter on Space.
6. Ibid. Chapter on Space.
7. Preston-Dunlop, V., *The Nature of the Embodiment of Choreutic Units in Contemporary Choreography*
   Publ.: Laban Center for Movement and Dance, London (1981), page 183-194

8. Dell, Cecily, *A Premier for Movement Description*
Publ.: Dance Notation Bureau, New York 1977, page 22

9. Preston-Dunlop, Veronica, *Dance is a Language isn't, it?*
Publ.: Laban Center for Movement and Dance, London, 3rd ed. 1987, chapter on Dynamic.

10. Ibid. Chapter on Relationship.

Chapter 7

Basic Characteristics of the Five Latin Dances

1. Meri, La, *Total Education In Ethnic Dance*
Publ.: Marcel Dekker, New York 1977, page 28

Characterization

1. Laban, Rudolf, *Mastery of Movement*
Publ.: MacDonald & Evans. Plymouth 1980, page 104

2. Ibid. page 114.

3. Laban, Rudolf, *The Mastery of Movement*
Publ.: McDonald & Evans Ltd., 4th ed., London 1980, page 78/79.

4. Ibid. page 115.

The Dramatic Conflict In Latin

1. Laban, Rudolf, *Mastery of Movement*
Publ.: MacDonald & Evans, Plymouth 1980, page 3

Chapter 8

Beyond Physicality

1. Jacob, Ellen, *Dancing*
Publ.: Addison Wesley, London 1979, page 27.

You and Your Partner

1. Laban, Rudolf, *Mastery of movement*
Publ.: MacDonald & Evans, Plymouth 1980, page 80.

2. Crompton, Paul, *T'ai Chi For Two*
Publ.: Shambhala, Boston 1989, page 5.

3. Ibid. page 6.

4. Ibid. page 26.

Balance – an Unstable Stability

1. Laird, Walter, *Technique of Latin Dancing* (IDTA)
Publ.: David Green Ltd., Kettering, Northamptonshire 1983, page 17.

Rhythm

1. Hawkins, A. M., *Creating through Dance*
Publ.: Dance Horizons Books, New Jersey 1969, page 52.

Appendix

Expression – Feeling – Emotion

1. Hanna, J. C., *The Performer-Audience Connection*
Publ.: University of Texas Press, Austin 1983, page 35.

2. Langer, Susanne K., *Feeling and Form*
Publ.: Charles Scribners's Sons, New York 1953.

3. Banes, Sally, *Terpsichore in Sneakers*
Publ: Wesleyan Connecticut 1987, page 43.

4. Switzer, Ellen / Taylor, Paul, *Horizons in American Dance*
(in Quintect by Moira Hodgson)
Publ.: Atheneum, New York 1982, page 114

5. Brownell, Catherine, *Dance Theatre Journal*, Volume 8, Spring 1991, *Petronio and his political body*, page 20.

Creativity

1. Ellfeldt, Lois, *Dance from Magic to Art*
Publ.: C.Brown, Texas 1976, page 167

2. Ibid. page 168

3. Reid, Harold Rugg, *Imagination*
Publ.: Harper and Row, New York 1963, page 298

4. Ellfeldt, Lois, *Dance from Magic to Art*
Publ.: C. Brown, Texas 1976, page 169

Bibliography

ARTICLES

Louis Arnaud Reid, *Sport, The Aesthetic and Art*, 1976

Louis Arnaud Reid, *Movement and Meaning*, 1970

Gordon Curl, *The Skilful – a Major Sector of the Aesthetic*, Fall 1973 Vol. 32. No. 1

MAGAZINES

Dance Beat, Miami, USA

Dance News, Godalmy/Surrey, Great Britain

Tanzspiegel, Neu-Isenburg, Germany

Brownell, Catherine, *Petronio and his political body* Dance Theatre Journal, London, Volume 8, Spring 1991

BOOKS

Adshead, J., *Dance History*. Publ.: Dance Books, London 1983

Argyle, Michael, *Bodily Communication*. Publ.: Methuen & Co. Ltd., New York 1975, 2nd ed., preface

Austin, R., *Images of the Dance*. Publ.: Vision Press Limited, London 1975

Banes, Sally, *Terpsichore in Sneakers*. Publ.: Wesleyan Connecticut 1987

Bartenieff, I., *Body Movement*. Publ.: BS Press, New-York 1986

Beatty, Patricia, *Form Without Formula*. Publ.: Press of Terpsichore Limited, Toronto 1985

Bellido, R. T., *Kandinsky*. Publ.: Bracken Books, London 1987

Billiet, H., *De Klank van de Houten Druppel.*
Publ.: Brt, Belgium 1988

Brinson, Peter, *The Changing Nature of Dance Studies.*
Dance Studies, ed. Roderyk Lange, Vol. 3, 1978/9

Brown. J. M., *The Vision of Modern Dance.*
Hanya Holm Speaks, page 73.
Publ: Princeton Book Company, Princeton 1979.

Buckman, P., *Let's Dance.*
Publ.: Paddington Press USA 1978

Chodorow, Joan, *Dance Theraphy & Depth Psychology.*
Publ.: Routledge & Kegan Paul, London 1991

Copeland, R., *What is Dance?*
Publ.: Oxford Press 1983

Crompton, Paul, *T'ai Chi For Two.*
Publ: Shambhala, Boston 1989

Dell, Cecily, *A Premier for Movement Description.*
Publ.: Dance Notation Bureau, New York 1977

Doubler, N. H., *Dance a Creative Art Experience.*
Publ.: The University of Wisconsin Press, 1957 (83)

Ellfeldt, Lois, *Dance from Magic to Art.*
Publ.: C. Brown, Texas/USA 1976

Fraleigh, S. H., *Dance and the Lived Body.*
Publ.: Pittsburgh Press, Pennsylvania 1987

Hanna, Judith Lynne, *To Dance is Human.*
Publ.: University of Chicago Press 1979

Hanna, Judith Lynne, *The Performer-Audience Connection.*
Publ.: University of Texas Press, Austin 1983

Hanna, Judith Lynne, *Dance, Sex and Gender.*
Publ.: University of Chicago Press, 1986 (88)

Hayes, E., *Introduction to the Teaching of Dance.*
Publ.: Krieger, New York 1980

Huang, Al, *The Essence of TaI JI.*
Publ.: Celestial Arts California 1987

Jacob, Ellen, *Dancing.*
Publ: Addison Wesley, London 1979

Johnstone, M. S., *The Phenomenology of Dance.*

Publ.: Dance Books, London 1966

Laban, Rudolf, *Choreutics.*
Publ.: MacDonald & Evans, London 1966

Laban, Rudolf, *Mastery of Movement.*
Publ.: MacDonald & Evans, Plymouth 1980

Laird, Walter, *Technique of Latin Dancing* (IDTA, printed by David Green Ltd, Kettering, Northamtonshire 1983)

Lamb, Warren / Watson, Elizabeth, *Body Code. The Meaning of Movement.*
Publ.: Princeton Book Company, Princeton 1979

Langer, Susanne K., *Feeling and Form.*
Publ.: Charles Scribners's Sons, New York 1953

Langer, Susanne K., *Problems of Art.*
Publ.: Charles and Son's New York 1957

Maerin, John, *Introduction to the Dance.*
Publ.: W. W. Norton & Company Inc., New York 1939

Martin, J., *The Dance in Theory.*
Publ.: Princeton Pennington 1965

Martin, John, *The Dance in Theory*
Publ.: Dance Horizons, Princeton/N.Y. 1965

Meri La, *Total Education in Ethnic Dance.*
Publ.: Marcel Dekker, New York 1977

North, M., *Personality Assessment through Movement.*
Publ.: MacDonald & Evans, Plymouth 1972

Peters, R. S., *What is an Educational Process?*
In: R.S. Peters, *Concept of Education.*
Publ.: Routledge and Kegan Paul, London 1967

Preston-Dunlop, Veronica, *A Handbook for Dance in Education.*
Publ.: Longman Group, Essex 1980

Preston-Dunlop, Veronica, *Choreological Studies: A Discussion Document.* Publ.: Laban Center for Movement and Dance (internal Publication)

Preston-Dunlop, Veronica, *Dance is a Language, isn't it?*
Publ.: Laban Center, London, 3rd ed. 1987

Reid, Harold Rugg, *Imagination.*
Publ: Harper and Row, New York 1963

Reid, Louis Arnaud, *Ways of Understanding and Education.*
Publ.: Heineman Books, London 1986

Reid, Louis Arnaud, Article on Sport.
In: The Aesthetic and Art, 1976

Rijn, D., *Encyclopedie van de Sport.*
Publ.: Helmond, Holland 1960

Rogers, Carl, *Towards a Theory of Creativity.*
In: Anderson (ed.), *Creativity and its Cultivation*

Royce, A. P., *Movement and Meaning.*
Publ.: Indiana University Press, 1984, page 126

Sachs, Curt, *World History of the Dance.*
Publ.: Norton & Company Inc., Norton Library 1963

Schmidt, R. A., *Motor Control and Learning.*
Publ.: Human Kinetics Publishers, Illinois 1988

Switzer, Ellen / Taylor, Paul, *Horizons in American Dance.*
(in Quintect by Moira Hodgson)
Publ.: Atheneum, New York 1982

Shawn, Ben, *The Shape of Content.*
Publ.: Harvard University Press, USA 1957

Sorrel, W., *Hanya Holm*
Publ.: Wesleyan University Press, USA 1969

Taylor, Paul / Switzer, Ellen, *Horizons in American Dance.*
(in Quintect by Moira Hodgson)
Publ.: Atheneum, New York 1982

Walther, S., *A Cross Cultural Approach to Dance Criticism.*
Publ.: Cord Dance Ȑesearch Annual X, 1979

Williams, Raymond, *Culture.*
Publ.: Fontana Publ., Great Britain 1981